Off Her Rocker

*Written by Victoria McDaniel
for, and with, her mother,
Katherine Hamblin*

For you, *dear ones...*
who believe, or want to believe;
who love, and want to be loved.

Prologue
Mostly Love, Now

The stuff of ego with which we began, the mass
in the upper chamber, filters away
as love accumulates below. Now
I am almost entirely love.
—Hayden Carruth

What are old ladies good for? More to the point...
what is *this* old lady good for? Why am I still here at
the age of 92?

When my husband, Parley, passed away 15 years
ago, I thought to myself that I didn't want to linger far
behind him. I wasn't sitting in my rocking chair
thinking about how I wanted to die, but at the same
time, Parley had been my world for a long time, and I
didn't really see who I was without him being the
center of attention; the fun; the guide through my life.
He had left me in a comfortable place, with my
physical needs met. He had even gotten me a golden
retriever puppy, Roxy Ann, to keep me company. I was
working on family history and teaching a marriage and
family class through my church. But despite all that, in
those early days of being a widow, I rather felt that I
was biding my time until the day when I would pass
through the veil to the next life and be with Parley
again.

I have learned many lessons in the intervening
years. I have learned that I have things to do; things
that my Heavenly Father has preserved me all this time
so that I *would* do. I have learned that I have

something to offer beyond being someone's wife; albeit a very amazing someone. I have learned that even a lady who is "as old as dirt" (one of my favorite descriptions) can still be useful, render service, do the Lord's will, and even have joy. But the biggest thing that I have learned is that what matters most is *love*.

In the poem *Testament*, by Hayden Carruth, he describes the sands in the hourglass that represent the moments of our lives. He uses the lovely imagery of all our ego and immaturity sifting through that narrow passage and as it drifts into the chamber below, it has become love. At my age, I am living my remaining days in that bottom chamber. There are very few grains of sand left to filter down, and I can attest that indeed, what is left of me is almost entirely love.

My "Off Her Rocker" adventure began in late 2022. I went to church one Sunday and heard a message that inspired me to share my testimony of Jesus Christ on social media. I think that the idea was to post a photo and a message, but it was very clear in my mind that I should make a video, or reel. One of my daughters was visiting, and she said that she could help me post a reel to instagram.

She suggested that we should go for a drive up to one of our favorite spots, Lake of the Woods, Oregon, and in that beautiful place, make a sixty-second message. I hoped, as we posted that first reel, that my grandchildren would see it and know about my faith in Jesus Christ, and that I loved them. I thought to myself that if fifty people viewed that reel, then I would be happy that I had shared my message with those fifty people. To my surprise, that reel had 200 views.

I was not only pleased with 200 views... I was *finished*. I believed I had done what my Heavenly Father wanted me to do, and posted my testimony to social media. But a month or two later, when that same daughter was visiting again, I had the thought come to my mind that I was supposed to make another reel. This time, I was supposed to talk about being ninety years old and still having a testimony of Jesus Christ, and that once again, I was to express my love... not just for my family, but now for all of you, too.

Off Her Rocker has been such an interesting experience, and it represents a period of rapid growth of my faith in Jesus Christ. I want to tell you why: Each reel addressed a subject that I was *inspired* to talk about. It is a little bit awkward putting my old self in front of a camera to talk about such personal things, but I did not come up with any of the subject matter on my own. It became apparent over subsequent months that I was definitely not finished, as I had thought after the first reel. But if I focused on the growing number of followers or popularity of the posts too much, or if I tried to come up with something to talk about without the inspiration that comes from the Spirit, then all of my ideas would feel wrong, or "off" in some way.

Until I felt a prompting to speak about a certain thing, then I simply could not put my words together in a pleasing way. I have even felt a great desire at times to talk about my particular religion and faith, but each time I have tried, the words would not flow, and I have been given to know that my purview is that beautiful faith and testimony in our Savior, Jesus Christ

7

that spans *all* faiths; the love that he has for each one of us, his children; and the love that I personally feel, not only for the Savior, but for each of you.

This book is not meant as a treatise on faith or a book about the Savior. It is not a detailed biography of myself. I have studied many things in the course of my life. I have pored over scriptures. I have received degrees from universities and even had a letter of commendation from a governor. I have taught school for many years and raised children. Painted. Knitted. Played the violin, rather badly. Made mistakes and overcome many of them. But at the end of my life's day, I find that I am only expert at this one thing, and it is what I have become: *mostly love, now.*

It is my hope that as you turn the pages of this book, that we can have fun together. I want us to talk about some hard things. I want to show you some of the things that bring me happiness. But mostly, I want you to know how much I love you. *Let us begin.*

Lake of the Woods, Oregon

I did not play in cool green grass
nor wade in a sparkling brook.
I never woke 'neath a sycamore tree
from a nap to read my book.
Those things were naught but stories
I heard in bed at night;
Even fairies seemed more likely
As my mom turned out the light,
For my days were always sun-drenched
Filled with mountains, rocks and sticks;
Tarantulas and rattlesnakes
And shoes too worn to fix.
I often wandered quite alone
In that vast university
Of wildflowers, caves and scorpions
And a sun-crazed dried up sea.
One day a stranger looked at me
Then slid her eyes away
I saw something like pity there
So I ran to hide and play
Now, I know she saw my chestnut skin
At odds with white-blond hair
She noticed thistles in my clothes;
Skinned knees and ankles bare.
But don't you make the same mistake;
Don't mourn a lonely child,
For I was luckiest of all
And grew up free and wild.
     —Victoria

Chapter One
Love and the Valley of Death

I want you to go back with me to my childhood. I know I told you that this was not to be a biography, but I grew up in a most unusual and beautiful place, and the magic of it seeped into my bones and transformed me in ways that I feel, even now, in these rocker days.

There are some places in our world that are so ancient; so vast; so wild and insistent that they become a main character in any story that is set in them. It is so with Death Valley. My childhood was sheltered by the Panamint Mountains on one side, and the Funeral Mountains on the other. My days have been marked by its vastness; by its complicated blend of abundance and minimalism. I am forever a child of the land.

My father was an engineer who built many of the roads for the National Park Services. If you have driven into Sequoia, Yosemite, Crater Lake or many other parks, you have traveled on roads that he constructed. When he was sent to Death Valley, it was neither a national park nor even a monument. There were no paved roads, and it was his occupation to construct quality roads leading in and through the valley from different directions. When the roads were underway and the area was accessible, Death Valley was declared a National Monument. My dad was offered the post as its very first superintendent. He would remain there as Superintendent of the Death Valley

National Monument for over two decades, and I would have the most unique opportunity to be born and raised in that magnificent place.

Very recently, a dear friend and her husband planned a trip to some California National Parks. They were most excited to tell me that they were visiting Death Valley, perhaps partly in my honor. We spent an evening where I told them about places that they should visit while they were there.

My dad told me once that people would visit Death Valley and stay three days and think that they saw all there was to see, but that if they stayed three weeks they would realize that they could never see it all. My friends were to be in the valley for three days, so I shared my dad's wisdom and then suggested some park highlights for them to consider.

When they returned from their trip, I had a feeling of great anticipation to hear about their adventure in my magical homeland. I asked my friend what she thought, and if she liked it. She said "I absolutely hated it. It broke my heart to think that you had to grow up there."

I really had to laugh, and I share this because it has been my experience that people are either captivated by Death Valley, or they despise the spareness of it. If you are reading this and have never visited the enchanted land of my childhood, I hope that this sparks a curiosity to see it, and I hope that if you do, it will capture your imagination and light a fire of adventure in your soul, as it always has mine.

Near Wildrose, Death Valley, January 2021

While I love Death Valley, it must be acknowledged that I lived there before the days of central air conditioning. Temperatures above 130 degrees Fahrenheit have been recorded there during the summer, and temperatures in the 120s are expected. When you live in the hottest climate on the earth, there are a few accommodations that must be made to survive that heat. Living on the valley floor in the summer months during those days of no air conditioning would have been not only uncomfortable, but also quite dangerous, so we moved to higher ground for the hottest time.

But even outside of the summer months, heat could still be a consideration. I have to say that for all the years I lived in Death Valley, I don't recall being miserable from heat. As a child, I didn't consciously give it much thought. I imagine, however, that my mother did, from time to time.

One of the customs that we observed when I was small, was that in the hottest part of the day, we would take a nap in our relatively cool and comfortable home in what we called the village, on the floor of the valley. That home that my father had built for us there in the village looked out at a steep hill that stood some 700 feet above the valley floor, complete with cliffs, overhangs, and loose rock.

One afternoon when I was about five or six years old, my mother was taking a nap, and my brother Ted and I were supposed to be in our beds as well. Seven-year-old Ted, however, was restless. "Come on, Kay," he whispered; "Let's go." We climbed out of the window, for in those days we didn't have screens. Ted ran headlong into the blazing afternoon sunshine, and I was not far behind him.

We crossed the deep gulch behind our house and began picking our way up the steep hill that had always scared me. There was no trail, and the terrain was all loose rock and incredibly steep. I followed my brother as we made switchbacks; cutting back and forth, across and up the mountain. After some hard scrabbling, we reached a point where there was a heavy overhang that we could neither pass nor climb. At first it was quite thrilling looking down. I had a great view of the village where we and the park staff lived, and a panoramic view of all the surrounding mountains. But as I looked down, the thrill quickly passed. Our home looked very tiny and far, far away, and fear crept over me. We were so high and it was a very long way down the mountain.

Bored of our adventure, Ted started back down. There were no trails, but he was able to run down faster than the crumbling ground and loose rocks, as one sometimes can on a hill. He yelled at me to follow, but I was small and I was terrified. I had made myself a little shelf in the rocks where my feet would not slip, and I could not leave that tiny island of safety.

When Ted realized that I was stuck on that mountain, he knew he was in awful trouble. He had to go and wake up Mom, and tell her that I was hanging on the cliff up above the house. She immediately called my dad and the chief ranger, and they knew that someone had to go up and rescue me. But where two lightweight children had scrambled up the loose gravel, it was much more difficult for the heavier grown men.

Much discussion ensued about who would make the ascent. I could see them congregated far below me, and I was convinced that I was going to die, even as I watched a young ranger climbing up to save me. They sent the lightest man, and it took an agonizing half hour for him to reach the overhang. I clung to his hand as we made our way to the bottom of the mountain. As I recall, as soon as I was safely in Mother's arms, I was fussed over, and Ted was punished. It was not the first time, nor would it be the last, for either of those things.

But it is interesting to me to remember that we were not scolded that we should never do anything so dangerous again. For all of my childhood, we were permitted to explore freely and unsupervised. My father was a true adventurer at heart, and he seemed the embodiment of the wild valley. I think that he wanted us to feel as at home on this beautiful earth as he was.

But that day also stood out to me as a time where I felt protected. No matter what predicaments I got into, help would come. I was small then, but I knew that I was protected by both earthly and heavenly parents who loved me and would not leave me hanging on the side of a cliff.

Death Valley, January 2021

Chapter 2
Love and a '36 Buick LaSalle

A flower doesn't think of competing
with the flower next to it,
it just blooms.
   —Zen Shin

Within the four million acres of land that comprise Death Valley National Park can be found the lowest elevation in North America: Badwater Basin dips to 282 feet, or 86 meters, below sea level. The highest point in Death Valley is Telescope Peak in the Panamint Mountain Range, at 11,043 feet. As I mentioned previously, in order to survive the summer heat in the valley, accommodations had to be made. My father had a summer home built for our family high in the Funeral Mountains in Wildrose, where the elevation was over 6,000 feet. The temperatures were much cooler and the vistas were incredible. Standing on our front doorstep we were surrounded by the beautiful Funeral Mountain range and we could gaze across to the Sierra Mountain range with a breathtaking view of Mt. Whitney.

We moved to Wildrose in May each year when my brother's school year ended, and then moved back to the floor of the valley in September just before school started again. It was during one of those transitional periods of moving up to Wildrose the summer I was to turn five years old, when my idyllic childhood was permanently altered.

During our moves, we would make several of the hour-long drives from one house to the other in our family's 1936 LaSalle to transport our belongings. On one of these trips, my mother and I were driving through an isolated area between the two homes, and the car tire had a blowout.

In 1937 there were no such things as safety glass or seat belts. Even though we were probably not going very fast, the steepness of the narrow road and the force of the blowout caused our car to roll a couple of times. After the final horrifying roll, we landed upright with my face stuck in the windshield. Mother pulled me to safety and then did her best to extricate the shards of glass from my face. That is the last thing I remember until I woke up on a table in the valley with the California Conservation Corps. medic bandaging my face for a trip to the nearest surgeon, which was several hours away in San Bernardino.

My upper lip was entirely severed from my face, hanging by a quarter-inch flap of tissue remaining on the right side. There was a gash that extended from my forehead down my left cheek, thankfully just barely avoiding my left eye. My mother must have been devastated at the damage that had been done, and probably blamed herself even though it was not her fault.

Emergency plastic surgery reattached my lip that awful night, but the resulting scars and scar tissue were absolutely devastating to behold. I avoided looking in a mirror for many years after that, and I remember that the first time I saw a photo of myself, I was horrified. Aside from all the cut damage, my lip was pushed out at an unnatural angle as though I had a permanent sneer.

When I was 12 years old, a revisionary plastic surgery helped, particularly with the bulging scar tissue and the structure of my lip. But it didn't do much to help my self-image. When I looked in the mirror, all I saw was that I was terribly disfigured and would never be pretty.

When it came to my attitude, this was such a formative experience. As a little girl, I was convinced that wherever I went, people were looking at me, judging me, and finding me ugly and inadequate.

People visited us at Death Valley frequently. As superintendent of the park, my father hosted many visitors and even celebrities. Movie stars came to film westerns; wealthy philanthropists visited the park; sometimes political leaders; and my mother would often prepare dinner parties.

I dreaded these interactions, and when company was present, I would literally hide. I spent a fair amount of my very young years hiding in my mother's closet and when they would call for me, I would not come out. I was drowning in self-pity.

On the occasions where I had to be around people, what I remember was that they would comment to my parents about how improved my face was; that the surgeries had helped, and that I was healing. Rather than finding their words to be encouraging, I found them demeaning, condescending and even dishonest.

There are experiences in our lives that are are so visceral that we let them define us, at least for a time. In my case, there was "before the accident" and "after the accident." I am sure we all have these events, but this one stood out for me like Mt. Whitney rising up out of the Badlands. One day I was a beautiful sun-kissed towhead, and the next I was disfigured. I was sure that I was a tragedy.

But I wasn't, really. My family didn't treat me like I was a tragedy. Much of what I learned about positive attitude, I learned from my mother. She told me many times: never look back. If you want to look back for a little history, then do that. But never go back into the past to live the bad things over.

Mother loved taking care of the house and cooking; caring for her family. She displayed an incredible amount of confidence and perseverance, stepping outside her comfort zone to help represent my father and the Park itself by being something of a park matron.

My mother never told me to change my attitude, but she exemplified living a positive and productive life. I didn't realize this as a child, as a young mother, or even in my prime years, but as I reflect in recent days, I am convinced that my mother's attitude was even more formative in my life in a positive way, than my accident was, negatively. She truly taught me by the way she always looked hopefully toward the future and never looked backward in sorrow. I didn't realize it at the time, but she was teaching me that serving others and showing unconditional love was the best way to improve my own self-esteem and my attitude.

I would like to say that I learned this powerful lesson while I was yet a young girl, but that is not the case. Learning to love myself and others is a journey that I have been on for these nine decades. Finally, I am "mostly love now," but it has taken me my whole long life to get here. It is my hope that you are a faster learner than I have been.

Remember that sweet poem by Zen Shin: A flower does not try to compete with other flowers in the field. It turns its face to the sun, and in that warmth, it blooms. You are that flower. I love you!

...For the Lord seeth not as man seeth, for man looketh on the outward appearance; but the Lord looketh on the heart. —1 Samuel 16:7

Some time ago I read a story called "The Fisherman" by an unknown author, and it resonated with me because of my facial disfigurement as a child. It goes like this:

Our house was directly across the street from the entrance of a popular hospital in the city. We had a two-story home. We lived downstairs and rented the upstairs rooms to out-patients at the clinic. One summer evening, as I was fixing supper, there was a knock at the door. I opened it to see a truly awful looking man.

"Why, he's hardly taller than my eight-year-old," I thought as I stared at the stooped, shriveled body. The most appalling thing was his face—lopsided from swelling, red and raw. Yet his voice was pleasant as he said, "Good evening. I've come to see if I might have a room for just one night. I came from the eastern shore for a treatment this morning and there's no bus until tomorrow morning."

He told me he'd been hunting for a room since noon, but that he had no success as no one seemed to have a room. "I guess it's my face. I know it looks terrible, but my doctor says with a few more treatments…"

For a moment I hesitated, but his next words convinced me: "I could sleep in this rocking chair on the porch. My bus leaves early in the morning." I told him we would find him a bed, but to rest on the porch.

I went inside and finished getting supper. When we were ready, I asked the old man if he would join us. "No, thank you. I have plenty," was his reply, as he held up a brown paper bag. When I had finished the dishes, I went out on the porch to talk with him for a few minutes.

It didn't take a long time to see that this old man had an over-sized heart crowded into that tiny body. He told me he fished for a living to support his daughter, her five children and her husband, who was hopelessly crippled from a back injury.

He didn't tell it by way of complaint; in fact, every other sentence was prefaced with a thanks to God for a blessing. He was grateful that no pain accompanied his disease, which was apparently a form of skin cancer. He thanked God for giving him the strength to keep going.

On his next trip he arrived a little after seven in the morning. As a gift, he brought a big fish and a quart of the largest oysters I had ever seen. He said he had shucked them that morning before he left so that they'd be nice and fresh. I knew his bus left at 4:00 AM, and I wondered what time he had to get up in order to do this for us.

In the years he came to stay overnight with us there was never a time that he did not bring us fish or oysters or vegetables from his garden. Other times we received packages in the mail, always by special delivery—fish and oysters packed in a box of fresh young spinach or kale, every leaf carefully washed. Knowing that he must walk three miles to mail these, and knowing how little money he had, made the gifts even more precious.

When I received these little remembrances, I often thought of a comment our next-door neighbor made after he left that first morning. "Did you keep that awful looking man at your house last night? I turned him away! You can lose roomers by putting up such people!"

Maybe we did lose roomers once or twice. But oh, if only they could have known him, perhaps their illnesses would have been easier to bear. I know our family always will be grateful to have known him; from him we learned what it was to accept the bad without complaint and the good with gratitude.

The writer of this story went on to add this message:

Recently I was visiting a friend who has a greenhouse. As she showed me her flowers, we came to the most beautiful one of all: a golden chrysanthemum, bursting with blooms. But to my great surprise, it was growing in an old dented, rusty bucket.

I thought to myself, "If this were my plant, I'd put it in the loveliest container I had!" My friend changed my mind.

"I ran short of pots," she explained, "and knowing how beautiful this one would be, I thought it wouldn't mind starting out in this old pail. It's just for a little while, till I can put it out in the garden."

She must have wondered why I laughed so delightedly, but I was imagining just such a scene in heaven. "Here's an especially beautiful one," God might have said when he came to the soul of the sweet old fisherman. "He won't mind starting in this small body."

I love this story, and oh, how I love and appreciate the true disciples of Christ who looked past my own scars to see not only the person within, but more importantly, who I could and would be; my divine potential. I had angels in my life who saw those things for many, many years when I could not. I lived for decades needlessly avoiding cameras and trying to compensate for what I thought was a deficit. I think that I could have accomplished even more, had I not had the desire to hide from what I expected would be cruel eyes.

It has taken me many years and many more experiences to realize that what matters is not how the world sees me, but how I see myself, and how God sees me. I think that if each of us could try every day to see ourselves the way God sees us, that we would then, in greatly bolstered confidence, be able to turn our eyes outward, with less focus on ourselves and our deficiencies, and be able to lift and serve others, and be His hands in service of those around us. God sees us as his beloved, beautiful children.

Chapter 3
Love and Flying Lessons

Oh! I have slipped the surly bonds of Earth
And danced the skies on laughter-silvered wings.
—John Gillespie Magee

My family: my brother Ted, my parents and I—
were *stoics*. It wasn't that we didn't love one another.
It wasn't that, at all. My father was born in New
England in 1877, and in his way, had conquered the
world and was well into his fifties when I was born.
He was 20 years older than my mother, and she was a
quiet, elegant, well-mannered woman of 36 when I
was born.

I never saw my parents express physical affection
with one another, for it was not the way of my family.
Similarly, I don't recall my dad ever telling me that he
loved me. That seems cold by today's parenting
standards, but my father, while perhaps
undemonstrative, was certainly not cold, and I never
doubted that I was loved and cherished by him or by
my mother. I rather idolized my older brother, but our
affection took the form of shared adventures.

When Ted was about fifteen years old and I was
fourteen, my dad bought us an airplane, the first of
several. He loved airplanes and in his earlier years had
flown extensively in a Jenny, which was a very popular
biplane of the time made by Glenn Curtiss Aeroplane
Company of Hammondsport, New York. To my
recollection, he never flew *our* planes, though. He

bought them for Ted and me. This first airplane was an Aeronca, and we were to learn to fly it.

On a Saturday my dad drove Ted and me to the beautiful mountain town of Ridgecrest, California. We pulled into a flight school, and Ted and I strapped ourselves into a small aircraft for our first flying lesson of many. The trainer planes were built with no doors, so they were open to the air on both sides. This was disconcerting, as we were only held in by our seatbelts, and it was quite a feeling when the ground would rush up to meet us.

It's kind of interesting to put this into a historical perspective, as it was 1943 and World War II had ushered in a huge surge of flying. In 1931, military pilots were being trained at a maritime rate of about 500 pilots per year, almost exclusively out of Randolph Air Force Base in Texas.

Seeing war on the horizon, the U.S. Air Corps had commissioned 11 civilian flight schools across the country, which were then run by the government, several of which were in the high desert of California, quite near Ridgecrest. Beginning in about 1939, the Air Corps increased their pilot training goals first to 12,000 per year, then to 30,000 and then 50,000.

After the bombing of Pearl Harbor by Japan in 1941, there arose a near-frenzy of pilot training, and at its peak, almost 100,000 pilots graduated from those schools. The program was phased out rapidly, however, and ended in about 1943. So I can imagine that by my fourteenth year there were a lot of flight schools in the high desert looking to supplement business that had dried up rather suddenly.

So Ted and I began to learn to fly. My father drove us to Ridgecrest every Saturday for many weeks that year. We continued our lessons until Ted received his commercial pilot license, and until I had flight-soloed so that I could fly anywhere I wanted. By then Ted was 17, and I was almost 16. That was when the lessons ended and the adventures began.

I have to say at this point in my story, that God must certainly have had a purpose for Ted and me. We were no strangers to peril. We had, for all our young lives, wandered fearlessly in that giant desert full of cliffs and scorpions and other hazards. In fact, by the time Ted was about twelve years old, he often carried a .22 rifle slung over his shoulder on our adventures, and he was wary enough of the poisonous inhabitants of Death Valley to wear tall boots. I, however, mostly wore shorts and lightweight sneakers, and would jump down into dark caverns where snakes loved to hide from the blazing sun, without a second thought or backward glance.

But where we had spent all our lives walking and hiking the floor of the valley some with a sort of truce with the indigenous flora and fauna, we were about to take our adventures up into the sky, where so many different things could possibly go wrong. We could crash. And oh, *crash we did*. As I mentioned, our first airplane was an Aeronca, and since we crashed fairly often, it was by no means our last. We changed airplanes several times during those years.

Our last plane I can remember was a Navion, which was built by North American Aviation in the 1940s. It was a single engine plane with retractable gear, and was renowned for the power it had in relation to its wingspan. We loved that little airplane. It was a beauty.

Death Valley was a perfect place to have an airplane, because in the winter we used the hangar and airstrip in the floor of the valley. The hangar and airstrip had been built a year earlier for guests of Furnace Creek and the Furnace Creek Inn. Ours was often the only airplane in that hangar.

From fall through the spring, we had boarding school. We both had attended the Death Valley Elementary School through the first eight grades. Our classmates were almost exclusively made up of Timbisha Shoshone Indians, who harbored no love for Ted or me. Ted took the physical brunt of their dislike and was almost daily on the ground in some brawl with the boys in the school. Their dislike of me was more subtle, but I was happy to skip two grades and move on to high school when I was 12 years old, where I was the only freshman in my class.

My parents, concerned for our education, and hoping for more social interaction for their introverted and solitary daughter, sent us away from Death Valley to boarding schools for the remainder of our secondary education. I stayed with family and attended school in Missouri for one year. I then attended the Brown School for Girls in Glendora, California, followed by the Duffy Girl's School in Fallbrook, California, from which I graduated in a long white dress with daisy chains around my head. So our earliest flying adventures took place mainly in the summers when both Ted and I were home.

During those summer months we would drive down to the Panamint Valley, some fifteen miles from our Wildrose home, and our plane was tied down out on a huge dry lakebed. I would climb into the co-pilot's seat and pull the strap over my bare brown legs and Ted was nearly always the pilot. After checking over the controls, we would taxi along the bumpy lakebed until we reached the speed for takeoff and then lift gracefully off the sandy ground and gloriously take flight. Most days we would fly for at least a couple of hours, sometimes stopping at the Furnace Creek airstrip for fuel.

We would lose ourselves for two or three hours in the adrenaline rush of lazy 8's and chandelles, as Ted loved to do trick flying, or aerobatics. It was eye-opening to see our childhood stomping grounds from above. Those who have never seen Death Valley would probably be shocked at how vividly colored much of it is, and how the sky can be the most vivid blues, pinks or purples.

Those were thrilling days. When Ted did not go out, sometimes I would drive down and take the plane up on my own, but I was not as daring as my brother, and I would usually not go far, just taking a little time to practice my flying and enjoy the views of the Panamint Valley before taking the little craft back down to the lake bed.

After having children of my own, I often wondered how worrisome that must have been for my mother, for us to drive off down the steep mountain, on the same dirt road where we had our accident in the LaSalle, also knowing that Ted and I were flying, and sometimes crashing, that airplane down in the valley.

One day I remember as we were flying along, suddenly we couldn't see out the windshield. The oil cap had come off and oil had sprayed out across the glass. It was quite exciting for Ted to try to land the airplane with almost no visibility.

Several times we were forced for one reason or another, to crash land out in the desert. While we had imagined the dessert floor as a flat surface, we found when we tried to land our airplane that it is all gullies and small hills. Whenever we made a crash landing, the airplane would have to be repaired before we could fly it again.

One weekend, a flying club had flown into the Furnace Creek strip from Los Angeles. There were probably fifteen or twenty small, expensive airplanes lining both sides of the landing strip leading up to the hangar. I can't remember why we had decided to put down there in Furnace Creek that afternoon, but as we touched down at the edge of the airstrip, Ted suddenly asked me, "Are you strapped in?"

I replied that I was, and he said, "Good, we don't have any brakes." It was too late to pull back up, and our choice was to either crash into one or more of those fancy airplanes lining the strip, or we would have to plow straight through the back of the hangar.

Ted chose the hangar, and sure enough, our small aircraft raced down the strip past all the brightly colored aircrafts and into the small hangar with enough speed to take us right out through the back. This caused quite a stir among all the pilots milling about the strip.

One other particularly fun memory I have of our flying days was when I was at Duffy Girl's school. Sixteen-year-old Ted was devastatingly handsome to my young classmates, and he had made arrangements at his boy's school to take a plane out— I don't remember if it was ours, or if it was on loan— but he would regularly fly an hour or so to Fallbrook to visit me. It was terribly exciting, because first he would first buzz the school with a low flyover to let me know he was coming to see me, and then I would drive the school station wagon to pick him up.

Ted had permission to land on an airstrip, which was really nothing more than the long narrow driveway of a well-known movie star of the time. The descent was between mountain cliffs that necessitated some very daring aerobatic maneuvers in order to line up with the tiny strip. I would drive Ted back to the school for a visit, and his dramatic arrival and presence was the source of much swooning among my classmates.

Ted went on to race motorcycles and cars, and to have many more devastating crashes than those rather benign ones we had out in Death Valley. He broke his neck, his back and just about every other bone in his body over those next few years, coming far closer to death than my parents could bear.

Years later he settled into being a commercial airline pilot which he enjoyed until he retired, decades later. As for me, I didn't ever fly a plane again after those teen years, and I let my license lapse, but I think fondly on those days for so many reasons.

I am not a thrill-seeker and have always had a healthy regard for my health and safety, but I think it is important to our happiness on this earth to be adventurous, each in our own way. I had already developed a great appreciation for the beauty of the earth and for the value of solitude. I have always loved to take walks and hikes in the wilderness of whatever place I have lived, but learning to fly and going on adventures with Ted was something different. It pushed me far out of my comfort zone. I didn't know it at the time, but I would need to leave my comfort zone over and over during the course of my life in order to learn and grow and pursue my dreams and goals.

Maybe the adventures of our youth are a training ground for life itself. Ted was born brave, but it was something I had to learn, and if I hadn't, I could not have navigated what was to come. I believe with all my heart that our Heavenly Father uses experiences to prepare us for our lives, and for the work he has for us to do.

When I was learning to fly, I became acquainted with the phrase "low and slow." With regards to flying an aircraft, "low and slow" is the recipe for danger and disaster and is the precursor to the dreaded crash landing. I have found since those days, that low and slow can result in stalling and crashing in *most* areas of my life.

There is verse I love that says "Men should be anxiously engaged in a good cause, and do many things of their own free will, and bring to pass much righteousness... [D&C 58:26] When I have pursued my life and good works with enthusiasm and a sense of urgency, I have avoided the pitfalls of poor self-esteem, temptations and bad decisions. Heavenly Father loves us and doesn't want us to fly low and slow. I don't want you to fly low and slow either. I love you!

Beloved, let us love one another; for love is of God; and every one that liveth is born of God, and knoweth God. —1 John 4:7

I want to tell you a story I have loved for a long, long time. I like to think it is a true one.

There was once a little girl named Annie who loved her mother very much. Making her mother happy was her delight. One day her mother needed milk and eggs, and asked Annie if she would like to walk the couple of blocks to the market all by herself for the first time to shop for the milk and eggs. Annie was so excited that she skipped out the door with coins from her mother's purse jingling in her pocket. As she took the porch steps two at a time, she spotted her red wagon, and decided to pull it along behind her, in case the groceries grew very heavy as she walked home with them.

Annie walked through the aisles of the store, placing a gallon of milk into her wagon, followed by eighteen large, brown eggs that she checked carefully to make sure none were broken. Her mother had taught her how to do that and she was very proud she remembered. On the way to check out at the front of the store, she found herself in the produce section and she spotted an enormous display of cool, crisp, green heads of lettuce.

Annie's mother *loved* lettuce. Hadn't she heard her mother say that she could just never have enough lettuce? Annie felt in her pocket for the coins and folded bills her mother had pressed into her hand—far more than she needed for a gallon of milk and some eggs. A lovely idea took shape in her mind. She began to count the heads of lettuce as she placed them in the wagon. *Eleven, twelve, thirteen…*

"What does your mama want with all this lettuce?" boomed the voice of the gray-haired store owner as he filled the large brown paper grocery bags to overflowing with the beautiful green heads. She just smiled, and as she started for home, her feet barely touched the ground. Her mother was going to be so happy and surprised.

But as Annie neared her home, a young mother pushing a stroller paused on her walk to turn and look very funny at Annie with her wagon full of lettuce. Then she noticed another neighbor, an old man tending his lawn, scowl at her as he saw her wagon overflowing with the lettuce.

Suddenly a terrible thought began to take root in her mind. Annie began to realize that she had done something very silly. She had spent all the spare change on lettuce, and there was no way her mother, or even her whole family, would be able to eat it all. She thought of her older brothers and how they would tease. But mostly she thought of her mother; her mother would be disappointed in her; maybe even angry; and she could not bear that. She would never be trusted to shop by herself again. Her steps grew slower and slower and her head was bowed in pure misery.

Annie's mother was watching for her from the front window. When she saw her sad little girl pulling her wagon so slowly up the driveway, she knew something was terribly wrong. Afraid that Annie had gotten hurt, she ran to the door and across the porch. As she started down the steps to meet her daughter, she saw all those bags of lettuce, and she felt tears spring to her eyes as she realized what had happened.

She hurried down the last few stairs and gasped and clapped her hands over her mouth in surprise. Then she squeezed Annie tight in her arms and put a big loud kiss on the top of her head. "Oh, Annie! How wonderful to have all the lettuce that I can eat! You must be the best, most thoughtful daughter that a mother has ever had."

Annie watched her mother scoop two of the bags of lettuce up in her arms and climb the stairs to the house. Her heart was so full of love for her mother that she thought it would burst right out of her chest. It was not until she was a mother herself, thinking fondly of that day with the lettuce, that she realized that her mother had loved her so much that she had rescued her that day; how differently her life might have turned out if her mother had criticized and belittled her and pointed out her mistake.

Many years later, when Annie was a widow and quite old, she was asked to teach a class of 10- and 11-year-old boys in church. Her pastor had been struggling to find a teacher who could handle these boys, and perhaps an elderly lady was an odd choice, especially since these unruly, disrespectful boys had driven away too many teachers to count. Even as she readily agreed to teach the class, he was worried they would be so awful that she would quit after the first day. But he was prompted by the Lord that she needed to be the teacher for that class.

The first Sunday that Annie met with the boys, she walked in and was almost knocked over by two of the boys who were wrestling on the ground. Others were loudly arguing about a video game, and the boisterous talk and laughter were almost deafening. They paid no attention to small, quiet Annie. In fact, no one even seemed to notice she was there. She could imagine how the other teachers had wanted to raise their voices and discipline the rowdy boys. But Annie remembered her mother and the lettuce, and her heart was softened by love and affection for them.

Quietly, Annie stood at the front of the class, smiling. She began to speak, teaching the lesson she had prepared. One by one, the boys began to listen. Curiosity brought a hush to the room, and soon they all sat in their chairs to hear what she was saying. In every lesson over the next many weeks, she found ways to show the boys how much she loved them. Within a few weeks, she had the most attentive and reverent class in church. These boys responded to her love. Love is a great power. *Love is of God.*

Chapter 4
Love and the Garden

*For God so loved the world, that he gave his only
begotten Son, that whosoever believeth in him should
not perish, but have everlasting life.*
—John 3:16

A lovely friend of mine recently lost a beautiful,
gregarious granddaughter to a tragic accident, and I
felt so sad to hear of it. She told me she was grateful
that shortly before the accident, she enjoyed a
memorable vacation with that young family and had
the opportunity to spend time with her sweet
granddaughter. As we talked, I thought of the little
girl's parents, and it struck me how very heartbreaking
our mortal lives can be. None of us goes through this
experience of living and loving, without experiencing
loss and pain.

When I was young, girls would often have a
special box called a hope chest, which they would fill
with treasures laid up in the expectation; the *hope…*
of being happily married someday. They might include
handmade linens or other household items and when
the young lady married, it would travel with her to her
new home. I always found a hope chest to be a wildly
romantic notion, and imagined filling mine with all
kinds of lovely handmade treasures.

As I have prepared to write this book, I have often
felt as though I am dusting off a beautifully carved
wooden hope chest from my youth. I raise the curved
lid and carefully lift out one parcel at a time. From

each parcel, I lay aside soft tissue paper to reveal an heirloom from my life. Some of the items I am eager to open, as they are memories of joyful times that I remember fondly. Others take me by surprise and they prick my heart; they are experiences, failures or losses that I placed deep in the chest, hoping that I would never have to look at them again.

I think that without this book, I would happily have left the hope chest in my attic, with both its dust and its contents—whether good or bad, left undisturbed. But I am happy that I opened it. When I laid many of those more sorrowful things away, I thought they should never again see the light of day, but when I look at them with these old eyes, I find that they are more beautiful than I remember; they are *redeemable*.

The Atonement of our Savior, Jesus Christ took place in a secluded garden called Gethsemane some two thousand years ago. I do not pretend to be an expert in theology, but even if I was, I believe that the Atonement transcends our mortal understanding. Attempting to understand it, though, is vital to our very salvation and our happiness here on earth and beyond.

In this beautiful, voluntary act of redemption, Jesus fulfilled both his roles—first as the Son of *Man*, suffering the very depths of the mortal experience, and second— simultaneously atoning for our sins as only the Son of *God* could do. In the hymn *It is Well With My Soul* by Horatio Spafford, I love this line: "For God has regarded my helpless estate and has shed his own blood for my soul." Without forgiveness of my sins, I am pitiful and hopeless, but the Atonement changes everything. Because of Jesus' suffering and dying so that I could repent and be clean; I am redeemed, and that is the most glorious, miraculous thing in the whole world.

The Birth of Jesus

He must have trembled when he heard the plan
And saw that his role was to die for man.
He would have to be born in a humble stall,
And take upon himself the sins of us all.
He would need to endure great suffering and pain
And his blood would fall as if it were rain.
He must have considered how hard it would be
And yet he said, "Here am I; send me."
Jesus was a god in that pre-earth time.
He'd created this earth and declared it fine.
We worshipped him there and revered his name.
Would he come to earth to die in shame
As a humble preacher with hardly a friend?
Would that be the way his mortal life would end?
But Jesus knew each of us before we came here.
He saw our desires and knew of our fear
But he saw the glory we each could attain
And for that He'd be born; for that he'd be slain.
So he may have considered how hard it would be
But gladly he said, "Here am I. Send me."
—Katherine Hamblin, 2013

If not for this sacrifice that the Savior made for each of us in the Garden of Gethsemane and his crucifixion and resurrection, we would be lost. We could never be made clean enough and thus never return to the presence of our Father in Heaven. But I also believe that in this terrible and beautiful event, Jesus suffered for *more* than our sins. The scope was so grand; so perfect and complete that he assumed *all the suffering of humanity*. The Atonement covers our grief and every pain, large and small. He suffered the humiliation of a small girl with a disfigurement. He felt the grief of parents who lose their youngest daughter. He took upon himself the plight of the child who endures unimaginable abuse; the guilt and remorse of personal failure or causing grief to another. There is no hurt too large or too small; no place in our hearts too far for the Savior's atoning sacrifice to reach out and gather us close… to soothe, save and redeem.

Without this assurance and reassurance, over and over in our lives, we could not feel the peace and joy that our Heavenly Father ultimately wants for us.

In the course of this book, I talk about things both happy and sad. I talk about things I have done that I am proud of, and I talk about failures that have brought me heartache and shame. These are are my legacy; they are the tissue-wrapped contents of my hope chest.

It is with intention that I place this chapter here, somewhere in the middle of the book, because that is where the Atonement belongs. It abides at the very heart of my existence. The Savior's redeeming sacrifice reaches back in time to heal and forgive. It settles in my heart every day to give me courage to do hard things, and it reaches forward to lead me, lovingly.

I hope as we continue, that you might view my experiences through the olive branches of the Garden of Gethsemane. I want you to feel the influence of that Atonement in every aspect of my words, as though we were sitting together among the flowering vines to talk with one another, much as the Savior went to the garden on many occasions to commune with his disciples.

That transcendent event that took place in the Garden redeems me and takes away the sting of shame and regret. It allows me to look at my own experiences with a fond and forgiving heart. It gives me courage for what is to come. And the sweetest news of all, is that it is available to you as well, because you, too, are a beloved child of God. I love you!

Chapter 5
Love and the Magic of Words

The Muse
A word is dead when it is said,
some say.
I say
it just begins to live
that day.
—Emily Dickinson

I have always loved the written word. I am endlessly fascinated with words like onomatopoeia, which, in case you are unfamiliar with it, is a word that sounds like what it means. For instance, "gurgle" is the sound water makes as it goes down a drain. "Snip" is the sound scissors make when they make a small cut. Aren't words amazing things?

I learned to read fluently before I started school. I read "Girl of the Limberlost," "Little Women," and I loved the poetic rhythms of authors as diverse as Dr. Seuss and Edgar Allen Poe. I became entranced with Charles Dickens' books at a young age. I favored them because of what he did with the language. Charles Dickens could put words together and make magic.

When I was a pre-teen, I had a New Testament. I don't know where it came from, because my parents were not particularly religious. I read it all the time, over and over. I loved the way the words were put together and I learned to love the savior at that time. There was a cave near our home in Wildrose that was filled with ancient petroglyphs, and I loved to take a book there to read, surrounded by all those ancient Native Americans who had come before. During that time, when I was studying and reading the New Testament, I had questions, and no one whom I could ask.

I remember many times kneeling down in the brush to pray for the Lord to answer my questions. I was so amazed at how they always got answered in one way or another. I wanted to know where I came from. Or specific questions like "Why did Jesus die?" Usually the next day when I would go back there to sit and ponder, the answers for those previous questions would be waiting for me, there in my mind.

Even in my somewhat feral wanderings as a child, I learned that I was never really alone. When I was about ten years old, I was hiking down a canyon with steep hills on both sides. I was walking along just enjoying the mountains, when all of a sudden I stopped and a feeling came flooding over me that I can't describe very well. I like how C.S. Lewis explained this feeling, where he said he was "drenched with joy." That was the feeling I got, along with gratitude; gratitude toward my Savior. This feeling, which I now recognize as feeling the Spirit of God, lasted only about a minute, but it has influenced the rest of my life. No matter what else ever happened, I could never deny that outpouring of love from God that I felt at that time.

In the summer months when we spent more than four months living in Wildrose, entirely isolated from any other human habitation, reading was my greatest delight. Each week, one of the rangers would drive into Independence to the library, and that librarian would choose ten or twelve books for me for that week. I would read those voraciously in preparation for the next batch the following week. That librarian really formed my basis for a love of literature, and I don't even know her name.

I have always loved mystery and suspense and a good romance. But to be a great book, there has to be magic in the words. The way a book is written is very important to me. Dickens' "Great Expectations" comes to mind. Jane Austen. I love a book that when I read the last page and close the book, I feel a great uplift of spirit. I also like a book that makes me cry.

One thing that was emphasized in my education was memorization. As a girl in school, we were expected to memorize many long passages in various subjects. This is not something that children, or adults for that matter, do much anymore. I suppose that when you have the internet and unlimited access to written words, it doesn't hold the same importance. But I believe that we have lost something because we no longer memorize.

Memorization is such a wonderful thing for keeping a sharp intellect. Memorizing the words to poems and hymns and scriptures and being able to recall them in the moment was such a strength to me in so many circumstances. I love some of the words to the old hymns. Knowing the words to hymns like *Come Thou Fount of Every Blessing, The Old Rugged Cross* and *Peace Like a River* has been so important to me. Being able to run them through my mind gives me so much strength.

I have set goals to memorize certain poems or scriptures throughout my adult life, and this practice has helped me to truly internalize many principles and gain a greater understanding of them. I remain grateful that I can still remember so many wonderful things and words and people, even at my age. I think it is important to challenge ourselves all the time. What passage of scripture or hymn are you going to memorize? Start with something small, and I think you will find it a habit you want to cultivate.

Along with scriptures, works of fiction and other prose, one aspect of the written word has always held a special place in my heart, and that is poetry. I remember learning the poem *Annabelle Lee* by Edgar Allen Poe when I was quite young, and the beautiful way that it flowed made me love poetry of many kinds. I am drawn to rhymes and rhythm, metaphor and simile, and all the beautiful and strange ways to arrange words into imagery. But mostly, poetry is the gateway to writing for me. Writing poetry has been a way for me to be creative, to express my thoughts and emotions, and to find peace, from the time I was young, even up to now.

When my grandchildren visit, I always have a few toys in the closet for them to play with. But I have always thought about the children and what I would like to share with them when they arrived. Most of the time the toys were the least interesting thing, because I could read to them or even teach them to read. I could get out paints and help them paint something. I could teach them how to draw a face. We could write a poem together.

Visiting Great Grandma

We paint some flowers
And read a good book.
We want to share
So take a look.
We wrote this together
Great Grandma and me.
We also drew pictures
As you can see.
Sometimes we're silly
And sometimes we're not.
We might write a poem
Without even a plot.
Or draw an animal
Without any ears.
The way we see it
Is how it appears.
We might write of Jesus;
We love him so.
And we love you, too.
We want you to know.
—Great Grandma and Brielle

For many years, I had a lot of fun composing a little birthday poem which I would illustrate with some quick drawings, and the poem would be enclosed with a few dollars for each of the kids' and grandkids' birthdays. I don't remember which year this was, but it was a typical one. One year I wrote about how "Grandma's cheese was slipping off her cracker" and another year I wrote about "Grandma being off her rocker" which is the origin of my Instagram name.

'Twas the month before Christmas
And all through the house
The only creature stirring
Was a little brown mouse.
Grandpa and Grandma were asleep in their bed
No visions of sugarplums danced in their heads
For they were asleep and their brains were dead.
Well, maybe not dead but it can surely be said
That all thoughts of importance from their minds had fled.
But the little brown mouse with a twitch of his ears
Jumps on the bed and Grandma arrears.
"What's going on?" she says in a twit.
But the mouse is long gone and she's in a nit
So she decides to get up and enjoy the day.
"Grandpa, get up!" she says. "Let's go play!"
But Grandpa says sternly from the side of the bed
"You'd better be thinking of birthdays instead."
So Grandma starts thinking of the kids she adores
And shuffles her feet across the cold floors
To get out a few dollars to put in the mail
So all you grandkids will know without fail
That we think of you often and love you a lot.
(I've slaved over this poem 'til my brain is shot.)
The day is gone and so is the light
So Happy Birthday to all and to all a good night.

I love how poems can be humorous and fun, or they can be spiritual in nature. They can bring comfort and peace when things are difficult, or they can uplift and bring the Spirit. This beautiful poem by my friend Jane Cherry is one that I have shared in my reels. I have loved it since the first time I read it. The tenderness in it makes me feel the Spirit every time I hear it.

Kisses

What good are kisses?
Only this:
Jesus' life began and ended
With a kiss.

I know that Mary kissed his face
And every other dimpled place
A thousand times when he was new.
I know the things that mothers do.

And near the end,
Remember this:
Judas betrayed him with a kiss.

But that betrayer's kiss, so weak,
Was not the last on Jesus' cheek,
For when they took the body down
And wrapped him in his burial gown,
Mary washed and smoothed his face
And brushed his tangled hair in place,
And long before they rolled the stone
She kissed her son and sent him home.
—Jane Cherry

A little over twenty years ago, my husband Parley and I were serving on our second church mission in the space of about ten years. Parley had been diagnosed with inoperable cancer and had been told he did not have a long time to live, but he was very determined to serve that mission, and it turned out to be an almost impossible task.

We were living in Manahawkin, New Jersey in a little beach cabin, with no neighbors in sight. It was a place that was so starkly different than anywhere I had lived before. We were alone in this little cabin and the tide would come all the way up to the back door. By the time we arrived in Manahawkin to begin the mission, Parley was already very sick. He was so weak that he began falling, and I was far too small to be of much help for his large 6'3" frame. He took one terrible fall where he broke his ankle. I was so worried about him.

One night I just opened up my journal and these words came to me and I wrote this poem.

"Be of good cheer for I will
lead you along."
These simple words have
enabled me to be strong.
During times when the future
looms dark and obscure
Trusting His promise
I know I can endure.
These words teach the gospel
in such a simple way:
His service to guide us
Ours to happily obey.
Oh Savior, it's already dark,
And night is coming on.
I'll try so hard to be cheerful,
And soon will come the dawn.
—Inspired by D&C 78:18

I was surprised and touched by how these words just flowed into my mind and made their way onto the page of my journal; they gave me so much courage and peace. But what surprised me even more was how I could go back to this page in my journal and read it over and find that same comfort again and again.

Before I leave this chapter about words, I would offer this one-liner that I have heard so many times before: "Everyone has a story."

Before my father passed away some fifty years ago, I asked him if I could write down his story. There were many articles written about him, but there was no biography, despite requests by some famous biographers of the time to write one. My father loved

T. R. Goodwin (top), Tom Day, Frederick Thurber

the sea, and in 1916 made a historic voyage in which he, along with Tom Day and Frederick Thurber, sailed a 21-foot boat called the Seabird from Providence, Rhode Island to Rome, Italy, marking the first transatlantic crossing in such a small craft. He was a musician and was at one time the manager of a world-renowned violinist. He won bike races in the late 1800s. He was a university-educated civil engineer and, as I have mentioned, pioneered the roads that traversed many of the great national parks.

So what do you suppose my father answered when I asked if I could write his story? He told me that he wasn't interesting enough to write about. I find it difficult to imagine someone with a more interesting and storied life than my father, yet he really thought that his life would not be of interest to anyone. I would propose to you that everyone does, indeed, have a story. We don't have to be famous or do anything newsworthy, either. I wish I had the stories of my father, my mother, my husband and my mother-in-law and father-in-law. I wish I could pass them down to my own children and grandchildren. I hope you will take this to heart and write your own stories.

If you think to yourself that you are not interesting, or that you are not a writer, or maybe you simply don't know where to start, I have a challenge for you. If you find yourself spending time scrolling on your phone, put it down. Pick up a pen or open a document on your computer, and start writing. Write a poem. Write a thank you note. Write a blog post. Start a journal. For goodness' sake, write a love letter! Write one thing you are grateful for. Write down something you believe. Just write. And then the next day, do that again. And the day after that. Before you know it, it will be a habit that will enrich your life. I know you can do this. I love you!

Behold, God is my
Salvation; I will trust, and
not be afraid: for the Lord
Jehovah is my Strength and
my Song; he is also become
my Salvation.
Isaiah 12:2

He is my Savior from sorrow and sin.
He opens the door and bids us come in.
He is the Solace for all of our sorrow.
He is the hope for our every tomorrow.
He is a Saint and all perfection,
From humble birth unto the resurrection.
He is the Source of all that is good.
I want to be like Him, if only I could.
He is the Sunshine that warms my soul
And only He can make me whole.
Jesus, the Son of the living God
The source of all power whose very name we laud.
—Katherine

Chapter 6
Love and a College Dropout

Skool is such a bore
I'm not going to go enymor
I no everthing i nede to no
So why evr shud I go?
I'll never need to multiply
And fraxions they just make me cry
Redings ok. I lik Harry Potter
But not the other books they say I otter
And speling - thats ezy
Anyone can spell - its ezy ~~pezy~~ ~~pesy~~ peazy
—Katherine

I thought, a couple of years ago, when I was "only" 90 years old, that I never learned calculus when I was in high school or college. I have always loved numbers, and the fun things you can do with them. I was always kind of sad that I never learned calculus. So I ordered an online calculus course. I went through it daily and it opened my eyes and my mind to so many new principles and ideas.

I have always found it sad when people decide not to learn certain subjects in school because they figure they will never use those things later in life. Well, I am "later in life" and I want to challenge this reason for learning—that it has to be useful, perhaps in some financial or work-related way. Every person doesn't need to learn every subject, but I think there are more reasons to learn than mere utility.

The brightest minds are the most curious. Highly intelligent people seem to find fascination and often, even joy in subjects that lesser minds consider to be merely boring. I have observed that lack of curiosity or an unwillingness to learn very often stems from laziness and apathy; taking the easy path. Learning is an eternal principle, and of course our Heavenly Father does not wish for us to be lazy or apathetic when it comes to learning and improving through education.

As a child, school came easily to me. I didn't have to study hard to do well and get good grades. My education was accelerated by a couple of years, and the summer that I turned 16, my parents sent me to stay with relatives who had a luxury apartment in New York City at Sutton Place, as well as a huge home at Montauk Bay, in the Hamptons of Long Island. This is now one of, if not the very most expensive real estate areas in the U.S. It was already an exclusive haven for the wealthy in 1948, the summer I stayed there.

My cousin, whom everyone called Demi, was four years my senior, but ever so much more mature than I, who had spent my sixteen sheltered years in Death Valley and small exclusive boarding schools. I was socially backward and rather introverted, and while I had made peace with the pale scars on my face, I never thought I was particularly attractive. All the clothes I wore at that time had been made by my mother, and because she was such an exceptional seamstress, I never felt like my clothes were substandard compared to other girls there, but I didn't give much thought to my appearance, and it seemed to me as though that was all other girls seemed to think about.

That summer spent in the Hamptons was a coming of age for me; it was meant to prepare me for college. The first week, I remember it being very important to my cousin Demi that his friends like me. I felt like a fish out of water. I thought I was so different from all those people. I had grown up in solitude. I had never belonged to a peer group. I was naive and I said silly things and didn't know how to talk to other young adults. At the end of the summer I looked back with some embarrassment, but I discovered during the two months I stayed with Demi, that those differences I found to be embarrassing had helped me to stand out and be unique. I had grown, to a degree, in social maturity and confidence. It is very funny to think of this now, in such a different time, but I remember that I even had a number of marriage proposals that summer.

One of the things my wealthy and kind relatives did that summer was to take my wardrobe in hand. Each evening during the week, Demi's grandfather David would get home from his offices in New York City and he would have the chauffeur bring in box after box of clothing from the most high-end department stores in the city, and each evening I would try on all the clothing. As I modeled each outfit for them, they would choose which garments suited me, and return the rest. By the end of my time there, I had a very beautiful college wardrobe tailored to fit my slim figure.

So, at sixteen years old, I began my freshman year at Chaffey College in southern California. I was armed with that lovely wardrobe from New York, some very tenuous confidence, and limited social skills. I don't believe I entered college thinking that I was going to be the smartest one there, and make a huge success. But I did think I could probably get by just fine without too much effort.

My first week at Chaffey I attended a student body meeting, and it was conducted by a handsome, charismatic young man named Lincoln. He was the captain of the football team and the student body president. I daydreamed about meeting him. Two weeks later I was walking home from school to my student housing, and a car drove up beside me and Lincoln leaned over to open the window on the passenger side and asked, "Can I give you a ride?"

Lincoln had been dating a popular, beautiful girl, and I had no idea why he would pay any attention to me. He had been in the military for two years and was older; I was only 16. But he saw something in me that I certainly could not. One day he said "Let's go to the mountains," and we drove up to Big Bear. We camped and he was very gentlemanly and respectful. He told me I was too young and he wouldn't spoil my life. He had me go to the football games and put me in a special place near the team. He told me he was going to marry me.

I remember going to his home with him one weekend to Southern California. He also took me home to Death Valley many weekends to visit my parents. Then at the end of my second semester there, he told me that he was going to be career military, an officer with a college degree. I had only the vaguest idea at the age of sixteen of what my adult life would look like, but I was convinced that it did not include being a military wife. This opinion was based on nothing and was the whim of a sixteen-year-old, but nonetheless I was completely determined that we were finished after that. It hurt me, but I broke up with him and had nothing more to do with him. He had been such a big part of my life and I cut him off completely and went to Yosemite to work for the summer.

I had done quite well my freshman year of college. I had earned good grades and participated in many activities. What I did not realize was just how much of that was due to Lincoln. Linc had been a good influence on a very young girl in her first year of college. He was a great student and I was motivated to do well when I was with him. But I came back to college the next fall with greatly decreased motivation and confidence.

I had become editor of the school magazine and I had all the scholastic tools to have a hugely successful year. But I never figured out how to make any real friends and I didn't have any motivation to go to class and turn in papers.

I got through that first sophomore semester with dipping grades, and began the second semester very poorly. I didn't want to be at school and didn't attend classes. I was looking at failing grades and personal failure in general, and ended up simply withdrawing from all the classes. I was a 17-year-old college dropout.

This was my first real taste of feeling like I had failed. It was not a good feeling, and it set me on a path of making some poor decisions. I would have many more failures in the years to come, mostly due to a lack of confidence and poor self-esteem. I wish, when I look back on this time, that I could go back and tell that 17-year-old girl that she was really going to be okay. That she should stay and put in the effort and make a success of that experience. Mostly I would tell her that she wasn't actually alone at all; that she was a child of God, loved and seen.

I can't go back and tell her those things, of course, but I can tell you, now: Whatever your sorrows and your setbacks, *you are okay.* You are not alone, so put in the effort. Stay and make a success of it. I love you.

Trust in the Lord with all thine heart; and lean not unto thine own understanding.

In all thy ways acknowledge him, and he shall direct thy paths.

Proverbs 3: 5-6

Several years ago when I was in my eighties, I learned that I had macular degeneration. It is an especially unpleasant diagnosis. It results in blurred or no vision, right in the center of the visual field—in other words, right where you are looking. Once damage occurs, whatever vision is lost, that loss is permanent. There are currently no treatments or cures to recover that vision. 90% of people with age-related macular degeneration have what doctors call a "dry" form of the condition, where cellular debris in the macula gradually causes vision loss. But mine took a different form, in which blood vessels grow under the macula, causing blood and fluid to leak into the retina.

With this so-called "wet" form of degeneration, I had to begin visiting a retinologist every four weeks and having injections directly into my eyes. I'm sure you can imagine the trepidation I had as I prepared to go in to the doctor. I thought to myself that I simply couldn't do it. I couldn't face lying on my back and watching that needle come down to pierce me right in my eyes.

I have always had faith that the Lord would help me. But could I trust Him to help me with this? Of course I could. And it was really the only thing that could bring relief from this anxiety. So I prayed very fervently for the Lord to be with me as I went in for these shots. Each time as I went in, I could feel the Lord holding my hand and giving me the courage that I needed.

A few months into these injections, I developed a complication. The doctor routinely used a speculum, which is the instrument that holds the eye open while the injection is given. After a time, the speculum was damaging the area below my eye, causing not just irritation, but sagging that exposed delicate tissues. I even had to have surgery to correct that.

I prayed about this again, and the next time I went in, I told the retinologist that he could perform the injections without the speculum. That is what we did for the remainder of my treatments. He told me recently that I was the only patient he trusted could endure the injection without moving. This wasn't easy because I had to watch that needle approach and pierce my eye without flinching.

We can trust the Lord with all our hearts. He will be there for us when we need him.

Chapter 7
Love and Rembrandt's Father

"Creativity is seeing what others see and thinking what no one else ever thought."
– Albert Einstein

I would be remiss if I wrote a book about love and happiness and God, but left out something that has brought me so so much joy for all of my nine decades of life. I believe we can be engaged in one of three occupations at any given time. We can either be consuming: that is, taking, breaking or even destroying. We can be inert, not doing anything at all for better or worse; or we can be creating: building, thinking, writing, painting, making music, making food, making anything at all… putting good things out into the world. We spend all the minutes of our lives in one of these three ways, but I feel closest to God when I am engaged in creativity.

When I was in my 40s, I saw this picture in a magazine. It was a painting Rembrandt made of his father. Something about it just spoke to me. I wanted it. Its million-dollar price tag was a little out of my reach, so I decided I would copy it. Salvador

Dali said "Begin by learning to draw and paint like the old masters. After that, you can do as you like; everyone will respect you." I don't know that that last part holds true for me, but I took his words to heart and from my youth I learned basic principles of drawing and painting. It took me four months to make my reproduction of "Rembrandt's Father." It still hangs on my wall.

I also love this quote from another painter, Pablo Picasso. He said: "Learn the rules like a pro so you can break them like an artist." I have loved painting and drawing throughout my life, and it has been hard for me to lose so much of my eyesight at this point in my life. Even a few months ago I was able to paint a triptych of winter paintings. I went on to make three paintings for each of the seasons. But my vision has declined very dramatically in recent days, and I can no longer see well enough to use my preferred acrylic paints. I went a couple of months without painting anything at all, but I was really missing that feeling that comes from creating.

I got a little leather-bound journal from my daughter's store that has thick cotton pages that work well for watercolor, and I began to fill all the pages with drawings and paintings. Because I can't see anything in the center of my visual field, it is very difficult to do any details. Putting the legs on a bird, I'm not at all sure if they are going where they are supposed to go. I am very demanding and critical of myself and at first I looked at these little paintings and I hated them.

But I thought about why I was doing it, and I realized that I love having that creative outlet, and since the paintings were for me alone, it doesn't matter if they are good enough to show other people. They are actually kind of special in their imperfection and imprecision and so you will see bits of them on some of the pages here.

Painting has been my especial joy, but certainly painting is not for everyone. There are so many different ways to be creative.

As I have mentioned before, I love to write; poetry especially, but I have written a couple of novels—one quite terrible, and the other, maybe marketable with a lot of editing.

After a trip back to Death Valley many years ago, I was told by the staff at the park that there was very little available history from the time I lived there; particularly about my family and what it was like to live in the park in that era. When I returned home I started writing about it, and was able to publish a short book called "My Early Years in Death Valley." Writing has been very important to me throughout my life.

I was taught from a very young age to do "needlework." A century ago, all young ladies would have learned needlework of many kinds. I learned to sew, although I never became the master seamstress that my mother was. I learned to do embroidery and to crochet, but what I really loved was knitting. I have knitted so much in my life that I didn't really have to pay that much attention when I was doing it. My husband and children used to tease that once we were watching TV and I was knitting and watching the show, and I fell asleep but I didn't stop knitting. It was funny, but I actually think it was true. The only problem was that I stopped following the prescribed pattern I was making, and reverted to a knit-purl pattern that had to be taken out back to where I had fallen asleep.

I have made a lot of different things with my knitting, but in the last 30 years what I have mostly made are hats and baby sweaters. I developed a baby sweater pattern that I have made over and over, with numerous variations. I have sold and given away hundreds of baby sweaters, and it made me really happy to make them. It is heartwarming to see pictures of beautiful babies wearing my sweaters.

I can't see well enough to knit at all now. I made my very last baby sweater last December. But I love my little pattern and hope that some of you might take up knitting sweaters. You, too, could be the baby sweater lady. It's a fun thing to be.

In the 25th chapter of Matthew, there is a parable about a master who was leaving for a time, so he entrusted his servants with his property. Talents were distributed to three servants, each according to their abilities. You may remember that one man received five talents, another three, and the final servant, one. As the parable goes, the master returned home after a long absence and required an accounting from his servants.

The man who had received five talents, and the one who had received three, both reported to their master that they had invested those talents, and in so doing had doubled the property under their stewardship. The master was pleased with them. In Matt: 25:3 there is this praise they received from their master: *"Well done, good and faithful servant; thou hast been faithful over a few things, I will make thee ruler over many things: enter thou into the joy of thy lord."*

Finally there was the servant who had been entrusted with one talent. He knew his master was exacting and that he required much, therefore he had been afraid of using the talent. Instead he had buried it away in the ground to wait for the master's return."Lo, there thou hast that is thine," he said, and returned the talent.

I doubt that the unfortunate servant was expecting what came next. The master called him a wicked and slothful servant and ordered that his talent be taken away from him and given to the servant who had ten talents. "For unto every one that hath shall be given, and he shall have abundance: but from him, that hath not shall be taken away even that which he hath."

I like to think that when we came to this earth the Lord entrusted us with many gifts, both physical and spiritual. Part of our mortal experience is to see what we can make of these gifts. Several of my children have developed great musical talents, which are often in great demand when it comes to community and church service. One daughter almost always had assignments to play the piano for various church activities, but one year she experienced a challenge of a different kind.

Her church leader gave her an assignment to staff the meetinghouse library during the hours of church. The library was stocked with various pictures, lesson manuals, writing implements, televisions for use in Sunday school lessons, etc. It was equipped with a copy machine in case that was needed. She was the best musician at church, and was also a very capable teacher. The duty of librarian once a week for two hours seemed like a waste of time. It didn't take any particular talent to check out a few items to teachers, and the rest of the time was downtime, spent reading or organizing materials.

I think my daughter was a little puzzled by this request, when she had some specialized skills that were almost always in demand. But she decided that she was going to make the most of that time. In fact, she was going to make it something more.

Each week before leaving for church, she thought about the time she was to spend in the library that day, and decided on a few things that she was going to do to fully utilize that time. She began by making a playlist of reverent music that she could have playing quietly in the background, so that when people came in they would feel uplifted.

One week she brought a sharpener and sharpened fifty pencils that were available to be checked out. Another week, a pregnant mother stopped into the library and said that she was feeling almost faint from hunger, and my daughter gave her the granola bar and fruit she had felt prompted to pack that morning. She made it a haven for a dad who was walking the halls with a crying baby. She familiarized herself with all the materials so that she could recommend videos or visual aids for teachers. She freshened up the crayons and coloring materials for the younger classes.

One day she got in her car to leave for church, and realized she had forgotten something. When she ran back in the house to retrieve it, she went to the kitchen and packed an entire meal of leftover chicken from the night before, energy bars, a banana and bottled water. She wasn't entirely sure why, because she would be home to eat lunch in a couple of hours.

That day it was quiet in the library, but one of the church leaders stopped by and introduced her to a man who had come to church that day from out of town. He had come for a job, but the job had fallen through, and for the last week he had been camping in nearby O'Neil Regional Park. He had cleaned himself up as best he could for church, and the church leader was helping him to fill out some applications for employment in the area. He was a very nice young man and had found himself in some very precarious conditions.

They gathered the materials they needed to fill out the applications, and just as they were leaving, my daughter thought to ask, "When was the last time you ate?" He looked a little embarrassed to tell her that it had been a couple of days, and she immediately knew what that huge meal in her bag was for. She told him she had brought him food and began taking all the items from her bag. He was so surprised and grateful, and my daughter felt like her calling of Sunday librarian was one of the most important jobs she had ever done at church.

I think it is so amazing to be blessed with talents in our lives. Some of us were born to dance, or to take beautiful photographs. Some have beautiful singing voices—I wish I had been blessed with that talent! Some paint, some write, some seem to be gifted at teaching or nursing or being a nurturing parent.

I know that there are some who read this who will think to themselves that they were not born with any particular talent. I hope you will remember that even the humblest of God's children are born with innumerable gifts. It is up to each of us to use the time we have here and to magnify it—make more of it than it is, and use it to put love out into the world.

In doing so, we are occupied in that noblest calling, of creating. We can do as Einstein said, and see the same thing everyone else sees, and make of it something new. I love you!

Choose joy

Hold a warm puppy against your heart
Kiss a baby's soft cheek
Get up early and watch the sun light up your world
Eat a hot fudge sundae

Chapter 8
Love and a Lone Pine

Laugh, and the world laughs with you;
Weep, and you weep alone.
—Ella Wheeler Wilcox

These next couple of chapters are the darkest of my life, and I want to tell you why.

For most of my ninety years I have been surrounded by loved ones who support and uplift me; family and friends who would never let me fall down by the wayside or be unbearably lonely. I stand sheltered in a beautiful grove of tall trees that allows the sun to shine upon me, but protects me and gives me loving companionship.

Even more importantly, I have my Heavenly Father who loves me. I have my Savior Jesus Christ, who sacrificed everything for me and who experienced all of my mortal woes. I have the Spirit to whisper to me and comfort and guide me.

During the years of my early adulthood, I did indeed already possess all those things, but I didn't realize it. I believed I was a lone pine standing in the high desert with cold winds swirling down from the mountains, pulling me this way and that. I thought I had to weather any storms alone and unaided. I had to bear any mistakes or poor decisions and stand alone with my shame and embarrassment.

When I dropped out of Chaffey College as a 17-year-old sophomore, I didn't want to go home to Death Valley, and I don't suppose my parents were keen for me to do that either. I had spent the summer after my freshman year working at Yosemite National Park in California, and I had heard while I was there about how amazing it was to winter there, and I wanted to experience that for myself. My dad arranged for me to go straight there when I left the college.

When I arrived I worked in the valley. I met a very good friend named Marion, who was in her early twenties, just four years older than I. Marion and I worked at Yosemite Lodge together. She was the hostess and I was the cashier. The atmosphere at Yosemite during the fall was very different than it had been in the summer and I loved it there.

Shortly after I arrived, Marion met and married a man named Bill. She and Bill moved to Big Trees in Yosemite to run that resort, and they took me with them. There was no one my age up there. It was a different sort of experience for me.

I had developed a love of solitary hiking from my childhood in Death Valley, and when I lived up in Big Trees I felt like I was in my element. People always scolded me that I should not hike alone in the wilderness areas of the Sierras, but remember, I was a lone pine, and I did it anyway.

I wanted to climb Mt. Raymond, which was a mountain near Big Trees. I knew I could go up and back in a day. I planned that trip, and Marion and Bill were very upset that I wanted to do that alone, and they told me I *couldn't* go. So, to avoid their disapproval I prepared a backpack with food and water the night before, and I slipped out in the dark before dawn. I reached the summit around mid-afternoon. It had been a steep hike and I was very tired when I reached the peak. I curled up in the strong sunshine at that high altitude and went to sleep. I slept maybe an hour, and when I woke up I was badly sunburned. I knew I had to get home because the fall days were short and darkness would come fast, so I hastened down the hill.

I love that feeling of running downhill. I would pick a place five feet ahead of me where I was going to place my foot. On that hike down, I picked the wrong place for my foot, and stepped into an animal carcass that was full of yellow jackets. They swarmed up into my clothes. I just took off running until there were no more bees. I was stung many times.When I got back, I got a severe scolding, but I was undeterred in my determination to hike alone. I was a lone pine.

The good thing about being a lone pine is that you are independent and can make up your own mind about things. Free agency is a precious gift; being able to make my own decisions and choose my own path is something for which I am most grateful. But what I did not realize at that tender part of my life, is that having free agency and independence is also possible when you stand in a grove with older, wiser trees for guidance, and it is much safer that way.

The bad thing about being a lone pine is that when you feel so very solitary, you can be swayed by the winds of life. They can tear at you, bend you and sometimes even break you. The next few years would teach me that.

When winter approached, they closed Big Trees because of snow. I moved down into the floor of Yosemite Valley, working as a cashier again at the resort there, a job that I really enjoyed. The Yosemite staff in winter was much smaller and more close-knit. I began to hear about a very talented ski instructor who, by all accounts, was headed for the next winter olympics. That was when I met Buck. He was tall, blond, handsome and very sure of himself. *And he was flawed.*

I was an inexperienced teenager and didn't recognize any flaws at that time, but in more modern terms, all the red flags were there. He had been married before. He was four years older than I, and had a son. Once I asked about his relationship with his son and I remember being totally shocked when he said he didn't have a relationship with him, and shrugged it off with the words, "Oh that was another life."

Buck was very interested in me, and, typically for me at that time of my life, I didn't really know why. He seemed very much admired by everyone, and I was naturally flattered by his attentions. He wanted to marry me, and I think in hindsight that I was swept up more by the romance of the situation than I was by love.

We drove out to Death Valley so that my parents could meet him. To my surprise, they immediately disliked him. I didn't have a lot of conversations with my parents, ever, and they didn't communicate well enough for me to understand why they disliked him so much, but their feelings toward him were clear.

My parents didn't exactly know how to tell me no; they had never really done it. It was not that they were overly permissive; they had just always thought it important that I make my own decisions. But for my relationship with Buck, they made a rare exception.

Mother told me they didn't like him and that I mustn't marry him. That was so uncharacteristic of our relationship for her to do that.

Looking back on this time, I realize that my parents' marked departure from their usual stoicism should have made me pause to reflect and, perhaps, to change my mind. But I did not. I was a lone pine. I went ahead and married Buck.

I can never regret that union because it resulted in two beautiful children that have been one of the great joys of my life, but it was not a happy marriage, even from the beginning. I think that had I chosen better for myself, and found a husband who truly loved me and was a partner for me, that I might not have been that lone pine anymore.

Maybe that was why I married— in hopes that I would not be so solitary. But I found in that marriage, and even in motherhood, that I was more of a lone pine than ever.

It became almost immediately apparent that Buck was not a man who wanted to be with only one woman. By the time I had my second child in three years, I realized that there was no expectation on anyone's part that Buck would be faithful. He would come in late at night or the next morning after being with other women, and I would do his laundry and keep his house.

One night I walked out through the huge trees in the forest of the Yosemite valley. I stood there under the stars and communed with my father in Heaven, and even though I was not a religious person, I felt His love, and a spiritual prompting that I needed to make a change; I could not live that way for much longer.

When spring came, there was a big Far Western Ski Association race at Mammoth Mountain. Buck won a lot of races and was very competitive. He was going to Mammoth to ski in that race. I went with him and we brought the kids.

As we drove along on Highway 395, all I could think about was my untenable marital situation, and as he drove, I worked up the courage to confront him about his unfaithfulness. I don't remember my exact words, but I said something like: "I don't know how you could be stupid enough to want to sleep with all these women."

I was watching his hands on the steering wheel of our car, and I can still remember how he took his right hand off that wheel. Without a word, he reached over and struck me hard with the back of his hand across my face. My world exploded in pain and shock.

I screamed at Buck to stop the car and continued to scream at him until he stopped and pulled over at the side of the highway. I got out, and took my small son and daughter out of the back seat. I had him open the trunk and transferred all the kids' and my belongings into one of the suitcases. He was standing behind me the whole time yelling at me that I couldn't do this. I was very quiet.

After the suitcases were sorted, I reached in the back seat and got out the couple of toys we had brought on the trip. With my suitcase in one hand, my two-year-old in my other arm, and my four-year-old son holding onto the suitcase, we started walking along the side of the highway.

Buck followed us for a time, screaming at me to get back in the car, but I did not, and at some point I think he must have given up and continued on to his race. I don't really know. But what I do know is that after a mile or two of trudging along with my exhausted toddlers in tow, I came to a sign proclaiming: *Welcome to Lone Pine, California.*

She opens her mouth with wisdom, and the teaching of kindness is on her tongue.

—Proverbs 31:26

Writer George Saunders said that what he regrets most in his life are "failures of kindness; those moments when another human being was there, in front of me, suffering, and I responded... sensibly. Reservedly. Mildly."

One time I was in a grocery store and I stood behind a woman at checkout, and as her groceries were rung up, she began to frantically rummage through her purse. "Oh no!" she cried quietly, almost under her breath. "I've lost my twenty-dollar bill!" She began looking on the floor and trying to retrace her steps through the checkout line. The look of desperation and panic on her face tore at me, but before I could really respond, she had bolted out the door without her groceries, for which she apparently could not pay, without the missing twenty dollars.

I opened my purse to complete my own purchase, and as I pulled out my wallet, I glimpsed the corner of a twenty-dollar bill just visible. I completed my purchase, but I have replayed that minute-long episode in my mind more times than I can say, but with a better ending.

How easy it would have been to drop that creased bill in the checkout line for that woman to find. There have been times in my life that twenty dollars was a small fortune—everything, really. A small act of kindness from me might have made such a difference for that woman who really needed it.

I realize that I didn't have much time to react in that situation, and that it wasn't so much a failure of kindness as it was a matter of processing time. But there is a term that is used most often in terms of personal safety, that I think might positively apply here. I think I could have benefitted by some *situational awareness*.

If our goal is to be kinder, and to make things better for people around us, then we should develop *service-minded situational awareness*. If we are always on the lookout for ways to be helpful and kind, whether we are shopping in a store, or at home making food for our family, or in a business setting… then when opportunities to show kindness happen, our minds and our hearts are already attuned to the situation and our kindness is *locked and loaded*, so to speak.

In the case of the woman in the grocery store, I might have already been reaching for my wallet if I saw the signs that she was experiencing a difficult life circumstance. Maybe the signs were all there, and she didn't need to lose twenty dollars for me to recognize them and offer to help her in some way.

My teenaged granddaughter passed away a few years ago from cancer. I know that my daughter and her family were the recipients of countless acts of kindness during that time, but they weren't offered as kindness or favors so much as they were just ways that people chose to express their love and support.

Her funeral took place at their local church meetinghouse, and a luncheon was provided after the service for the family. Knowing that my daughter would have all her children and several grandchildren visiting for the occasion, many from out of town, her friends planned the luncheon very thoughtfully and provided cotton candy and brought in a popcorn machine just to make it special for all the young guests. Other friends made homemade rolls and fresh raspberry jam because they knew it was my daughter's favorite.

We can't always take away the suffering of others, but acts of kindness, even as small as smiling, retrieving an item from a high shelf or recommending a favorite book can make all the difference to someone who is struggling. Usually what people really need is to know that they are loved, that they are not alone, and that they will be okay. If I haven't mentioned it recently, I love you!

Chapter 9
Love, Hepatitis and an Indian Reservation

A poor wayfaring man of grief
Hath often crossed me on my way,
Who sued so humbly for relief
That I could never answer nay.
I had not pow'r to ask his name,
Whereto he went, or whence he came;
Yet there was something in his eye
That won my love; I knew not why.
—James Montgomery

I know you must be wondering what happened to that young mother walking down the side of the highway down into Lone Pine. Did she stay in Lone Pine? Did she stop thinking that she, herself *was* a lone pine? I won't leave you in suspense.

I walked down into that small town from the exit, and found myself a payphone and a telephone book. There was a family that lived in Lone Pine that I had known since my childhood. They had a ranch with horses and a pack company that had brought the horses into Death Valley every year. I was friends with Barbara, Enid and Charles, as they were nearest my age. In particular, Barbara had been my friend since I was quite small.

When I woke up that morning, I certainly had not planned to walk down the highway with my two children and a suitcase. I had broken free from a terrible situation, only to put the three of us into a far more precarious one. My only thought upon reaching Lone Pine, was that I would make my way to the ranch of my childhood friends, and perhaps they would take us in for the night.

Heavenly Father was watching out for my small family. The first person who met me at the ranch was Barbara, and I poured out my story for my old childhood friend. Barbara was married to Tommy, and the couple managed many of the Mt. Whitney Pack Trains operations from there. They had three children under six years old, and to my surprise, they had named their first child Katherine. Barbara and Tommy took me in immediately.

Barbara advised me to call my parents, who would unquestionably provide for us. But there were two factors that made me determined that under no circumstances would I involve Mom and Dad, or even tell them that I had left my husband. The first was pure stubbornness. I was a lone pine. This was *my* disaster —my failure, as I saw it. I felt like I had been a failure and a disappointment ever since I left college with incomplete classes and poor grades. I could not ask them to help me.

The second, and most serious reason, was that my brother Ted had been in a near-fatal sports car accident in a race in Las Vegas. My parents had left Death Valley and taken a home in Las Vegas so that they could nurse him, and he was still not expected to live. Even if I hadn't felt like such an irredeemable failure, I could not have added to their burdens with my own.

Barbara presented a proposal which provided a solution to my immediate problems. She told me that they needed someone to run the store and cook for their pack station at Whitney Portals, and that it was ideal for me because I would need neither transportation nor child care. I was extremely grateful to Barbara for this opportunity, and she drove us up to Whitney Portals.

As we arrived at the base camp there, I remember seeing that tiny cabin that would be my home. I had such a feeling of peace as I stepped over the threshold. It was light and airy and felt like an oasis for my little ones and me, after feeling uncertain and unsafe.

The next couple of months were happy ones. Mt. Whitney Pack Trains hosted excursions that took individuals and organizations like the Sierra Club up Mt. Whitney. They would ride into Whitney Portals and I would cook a meal for them and open the store for business. I always got to keep my children by my side. I loved living in the snug little cabin there that was in the back of the store and restaurant, and I felt empowered, like I was finally getting my life back on track.

Barbara drove up one day when we had only been there a couple of months. She said that she'd come to pick up my kids and take them down into Lone Pine because there was a hepatitis outbreak, and the county just had enough gamma globulin for the children.

She took my two into town with her three little ones and had them all vaccinated. I was so relieved that they received the vaccine, because a few days later, Barbara contracted the disease, and as it was highly contagious, I got it from her.

That was the very darkest part of my life—the time of my greatest adversity. I went into the hospital and the only saving grace for me was that Barbara and I were together in the same room. We could have no visitors.

Nurses came in masked and gowned, but we were both critically ill and could not see our kids. But the doctor came in every day wearing a mask for his protection, and he was so kind. He would sit on each of our beds and talk to us for several minutes. Every day we had awful huge Vitamin B shots, which were the only treatment they had for the illness.

The sole, pressing thing that occupied my mind as I slipped in and out of fevered dreams, was the welfare of my children. I could not have contacted either my estranged husband or my parents, had I wanted to. My recovery was not a matter of days, or even mere weeks. Our lives—mine and Barbara's— hung in the balance for three months of isolation in that hospital.

Barbara's husband Tommy was a full-blooded Mohawk Indian. He and Barbara had been living on the ranch, but with my added burden of my two, Tommy had five children under six years old to care for. When it became apparent that we would be hospitalized for such a long period of time, Tommy moved back onto the Indian reservation near Lone Pine. He took the five small children, and cared for them with different American Indian families on the reservation.

We were in the hospital for those three full months, and they were the longest, hardest three months of my life; physically, spiritually, emotionally, and even financially: I knew I was running up huge doctor and hospital bills. Despite that, I was still determined not to wreck my parents by letting them know any of this.

At the end of three months, the doctor told us we could be discharged and return to Barbara's home, but only if there was someone to take care of us; we were no longer contagious but we would be flat in bed for another month. We were so grateful to go home to the ranch with Tommy to care for us and the children.

I may not have realized it at the time, but that was the end of my "lone pine" days; not the *town* of Lone Pine—I would actually return there as a school teacher some years later— but it was the end of my *being* a lone pine. I had been standing in a tall grove of trees that had expanded even to include, remarkably, an Indian reservation. I had never been alone, all along. The Lord had guided my steps down a lonely highway into welcoming arms and a community that cared for me without even knowing me.

It meant so much to have my kids back with me. I had worried about them nonstop during those months, and it probably would not have eased my mind to know that they were living with families on the reservation. But they were safe and sound, and we were reunited. Having hepatitis was one of the most terrible things that ever happened to me, but it was a great blessing. It was how Heavenly Father taught me some very important things.

My first lesson was a simple one: there was nothing more important to me than my children. I had been going along in my life letting things happen to me, but

I was a mother now, and so when I let things happen to me, I was also letting them happen to my children. I needed to take steps to be proactive and *make* things happen in my life, so that they would be safe and well.

It was time for me to really grow up. One of my notions as a sixteen-year-old in college was that I would not ever want to be a school teacher. It finally occurred to me that as a school teacher I would have my summers free to be with my children, and that it was the perfect occupation for me.

My second lesson was that I had to do whatever it took so that I could support my family. I did not ever plan to marry again and did not want to be dependent on my parents. I had to have a college degree and a plan. It is different today, but at that time, one could either do a minimum wage job, or earn a college degree. A college degree was a guarantee of a good-paying job.

The third and most important lesson was that I was not a lone pine, nor could I ever try to be so, ever again. I was not alone. I had *never been alone,* even when I thought I was. I was always loved by my parents. I was loved and cared for by friends who had not even seen me since my childhood. I was seen, loved and cared for by my Father in Heaven. He was leading me along a very rocky path; I could not see what was around the corner—but I was starting to have faith enough to walk that path and know that what was around the corner was happiness.

I hope you are developing that same faith, even through your adversities. It is such a blessing to know that God has a plan for you, and that it is so much better than any plans you might have for yourself.

Have you ever had the experience of flying in an airplane at night? I want you to imagine this with me. I have always loved a window seat so that I can look out for most of the flight.

For hours you can peer out the window to see nothing but inky darkness, broken only intermittently by a light flashing on the wing you overlook. Then the plane banks slightly to approach a city, and suddenly the blackness gives way to a grand view. Strands of glittering jewels sprawl against a field of midnight velvet.

So it is with Heavenly Father's plan. You may be in a dark place and unable to see it just now, but that breathtaking view is just around the corner, and each glittering jewel represents another blessing that Heavenly Father has reserved just for you. I love you!

Chapter 10
Love and Kerosene Casserole

I eat my peas with honey
I've done it all my life
It makes the peas taste funny
But it keeps them on my knife

One of the great joys of my life is food. Whether you are an old lady in a small household, or whether you feed a houseful of hungry teenagers, what you put in your body matters.

It is interesting to reflect on my relationship with food, because it seems that popular opinion regarding nutrition has changed constantly over the years, and even in 2024, medical professionals do not agree on all the principles of nutrition. It seems to me that they should have figured it out by now. But there are so many regimens that are in, out and in again. When I was a young mother, we were warned that we should never reduce our sugar intake without consulting a doctor! That advice, I'm quite sure, will never return.

I haven't always loved to cook, but I have certainly always enjoyed making food for people I love, and I feel just as much enjoyment when people make food for me. Feeding people— nourishing them physically —is an important way to care for them, and an important way to care for ourselves. Food can be so much more than mere sustenance. It can make memories; it can be art; it can express creativity; it can show love.

Sitting down together to eat as a family has become a rare thing in our decade. I recently read an article that talked about the "disappearing dining room," relegating meals to couches and bedrooms. It pointed out that people don't want to "waste" their square footage on a space that is only used for holidays and special occasions. This is such a departure from past decades when eating dinner together as a

family around a table was the norm. Sitting around the dinner table with parents and children and even extended family was often the only time during a day when the entire family would be together. Sharing meal preparation, conversation over food and the clean-up afterward is a unifying activity that I don't think we can afford to lose.

Parley hated my spaghetti. I don't really know why. I mean, I always liked it, even as leftovers. But he really didn't like it, and I learned to turn that to my advantage. If there was an evening that I really didn't want to cook, and was hoping to eat out, all I had to do was mention to Parley, in passing, that I was making spaghetti for dinner, and he was certain to say, "Kids! Grab your coats! We're going out for dinner."

One evening, however, we were all seated at the table having one of my dreaded spaghetti dinners. It was the 1970s, and this is funny to recall, but in the 1970s most dinners would include a jello concoction of one sort or another. They were often called jello "salads" and would have strange ingredients. But on this particular night it was plain old green jello. Of the six kids, the three oldest were teenagers, and there was some sort of conflict at the dinner table that night. My oldest daughter, Shawn, made an impudent comment, and rather than respond verbally, Parley took his spoon, reached into that gleaming, jiggling pond of green jello, and scooped out a half-moon of the stuff. He brought the spoon to a vertical position, and used the index finger of his left hand to turn it into a tiny catapult.

The perfect spoonful of green gelatin flew across the table and found its mark, adhering in a blob exactly between Shawn's eyes. After a collective gasp and a second of silence, the dining room erupted in an epic food fight, everyone flinging spaghetti and jello and rolls and green beans. No one got in trouble for that, especially since Dad had started it, but weeks later we noticed some spaghetti on the ceiling that had somehow been missed in the clean-up.

A whole genre of food that was popular when I had a young family was the *casserole*. The proliferation of casserole recipes was actually fueled by the Campbell Soup Company. Today if you want produce, you go to your local grocer, and you can find practically any fresh produce you want. If it is out of season in Maine, it will be shipped in from Chile. You can buy fresh cobs of corn in California in the winter; strawberries in Ohio year-round.

This is a development in the last thirty years or so. A few decades ago, home cooks relied on canned vegetables for much of the year, and casseroles were comprised mainly of easy ingredients mostly from cans, often featuring a canned soup base, combined directly in a casserole dish and then baked in the oven.

My mother-in-law, Dora, had a casserole recipe I particularly liked. It was something akin to chicken enchiladas, but used concentrated cream of chicken soup and evaporated milk as the sauce. I had not been married to Parley for very long, and we were to attend a "potluck" at our church. Potlucks are another blast from the past. Everyone would bring their favorite dishes and serve them buffet-style.

I really wanted to make Dora's casserole, so I asked her for the recipe. It was very simple, and consisted of a sauce made from equal parts of the soup and the milk, chopped onions and canned diced Ortega-brand chiles. The sauce went into three layers with corn tortillas torn into bite-sized pieces and shredded cheddar cheese, ending in the cheese that would bake on top.

I proudly took that casserole to the potluck dinner and placed it alongside many other casseroles and jello salads that probably had things like mayonnaise and chopped celery in them, rolls and desserts. It looked very tasty, *but there was a surprise inside*. The recipe had called for two cans of diced mild green chiles, but I didn't realize there was a difference between the mild chilies and the much-spicier diced jalapeños in very similar cans.

When it comes to the jalapeños, a little bit goes a long way, especially back then. I think that today we are much more used to eating spicy foods. Back then most foods were somewhat more bland.

The first person to eat the casserole dug in and had eaten a few bites before the heat caught up to him. He grabbed for a water pitcher and then yelled out, loudly enough for everyone to hear: "What'd you put in this casserole.... *kerosene?*" I was a little embarrassed at the time, but Kerosene Casserole—the milder version — was a staple in our house for many years after that, and it was never called anything else ever again.

I have a large family of good cooks. One positive thing about my health declining this past year is that I have had a great many visitors—children,

grandchildren, and great-grandchildren. And many of them have cooked for me. One grandson with three kids of his own cooks every meal when he visits, and then makes portions to freeze. I can enjoy one of his lasagnas months later. Good food can become a family tradition. I'm including a couple of recipes just for fun. And a challenge. Sit down at a table with your family for dinner this week. I love you!

Butter Rolls

1 ½ cups hot water (from the tap)
½ cup sugar
1 teaspoon salt
1 tablespoon yeast
3 eggs
½ cup canola (or other vegetable) oil
5 cups of flour, plus extra for kneading
¼ cup butter

Combine 1 1/2 c hot water (from the tap) with ½ cup sugar and 1 teaspoon of salt in Kitchenaid mixer bowl. Add the yeast. Combine three eggs and 1/2 c. canola oil and beat eggs slightly. Add to mixer bowl, along with about two cups of flour. Begin mixing at low to medium speed, and incorporate the flour a cup gradually to make a soft dough. Sprinkle with extra flour to make a little less sticky to work with. Mix for about seven minutes. Turn dough into buttered bowl and turn a couple of times to coat lightly with butter. Cover and let rise for 3 hours. Divide dough to make 35 rolls in a large cookie sheet or jelly roll pan which you have lightly greased or buttered. Allow to rise 30 minutes. Drizzle with ¼ cup melted butter and bake at 350 for 20 minutes.

Variations: This dough makes great cinnamon rolls. Combine ½ cup softened butter with 1 cup sugar and 2 tbs. cinnamon. After the three-hour rise, roll the dough out into a large rectangle and spread with the cinnamon mixture. Roll up and slice into rolls. Makes about 30 rolls, depending on size. Let rise for 30-45 minutes in a warm place, then bake at 350 for 20 minutes, or until golden brown. For orange rolls, substitute the grated rind of three oranges for the cinnamon.

Dutch Baby (Breakfast Pancake)

4 eggs
1 cup milk
1 cup flour
1 cup sugar
1 pinch salt
¼ cup (1/2 cube) butter

For Caramel Apple Variation:
prepared apple pie filling
2 cups pecan pieces
½ cup sugar
salt and pepper
vanilla ice cream (ice cream for breakfast!)
caramel sauce for ice cream

Preheat oven to 425 degrees. Put butter into ovenproof 10 inch skillet or pan. Place in oven. Meanwhile, in blender, combine eggs, milk, flour, 1cup sugar, and pinch salt. Blend just until smooth. When butter has melted in oven, pour in the batter and close the oven back up. Bake for about 15 minutes, or until brown on the edges and puffed and set in the middle. This is great topped with maple syrup or yogurt and fruit.

Meanwhile, for the Caramel Apple version, sugar the pecans. Prepare a piece of parchment (not wax paper or foil!) or a silpat mat. Place pecans in a skillet with ½ cup sugar and a sprinkle of salt and pepper. Heat on medium high until sugar begins to melt. Then stir constantly. The sugar will coat the pecans. After about three or four minutes, the sugar will be brown and start to smoke. When it reaches that point, stir quickly to coat, and then spread out on the prepared parchment. Let cool and harden, then coarsely chop. This sugar gets REALLY HOT. It can burn you like crazy! Just ask me… I have the burns to prove it. Use caution. When the baby comes out of the oven, cover the top with warm apples. Cut into wedges. Top with ice cream, sugared pecans and caramel sauce. Serve immediately. This makes a great dessert!

They might not need me;
but they might.
I'll let my head be
just in sight;
a smile as small as mine
might be precisely their
necessity.
—Emily Dickinson

Chapter 11
Love and the Prodigal Son

Forgiveness
Is the mightiest sword
Forgiveness of those you fear
Is the highest reward
When they bruise you with words
When they make you feel small
When it's hardest to take
You must do nothing at all…

– Jane Eyre, by Charlotte Bronte

My friend Larry told a story once that has always stuck with me. He was getting on the freeway in Southern California one day, and as soon as he entered the on-ramp he saw that the freeway was not moving, which is too often the case there. He had about 100 feet to merge, and then he would run out of ramp. So he either had to merge or run off the road.

No one would let him in, so he did what he had to do: he moved assertively in front of a pickup truck, essentially cutting them off. After he did, he looked in his rearview mirror and met the eyes of the man in the pickup. This person he cut off was *not* happy about it.

In fact, the man changed lanes and got next to Larry and started shaking his fist at him and making hand gestures, yelling obscenities. Larry thought about his situation, and decided to try to turn away the man's anger with a gentle apology. He turned and made eye contact with him and gave a rueful smile, and then he mouthed the words, "I'm sorry."

If you knew Larry, you might think to yourself, *that could have gone either way*. He is patient, but he is not the type to let people push him around, either. Not only that, but road rage is no laughing matter. The frustration and futility of terrible traffic drives many people to violence, often for something as simple as cutting someone off as Larry did.

What came next were an awkward few minutes when the freeway traffic did not move very much, and so Larry ended up driving alongside the angry pickup guy for some time. He said it felt kind of embarrassing — he really didn't want to look over at this person that he had offended.

But after several minutes he looked over at the other driver, and the man was making motions for him to roll down his window. Larry was a little worried about doing it... but he rolled down the window. As soon as he did, the man told him that he was so sorry for the way he had acted, and the things he had said and done. I was surprised that this story made me cry, and even writing it again brought tears to my eyes.

Larry said that we live in an angry world. *It certainly seems true. There is a lot of anger.* But I have come to realize over my many years that anger is usually the secondary emotion, and the primary emotion is hurt.

There is a true story I have always loved from a favorite book "The Miracle of Forgiveness" by Spencer W. Kimball. He talks about a woman who "climbed the heights of self-control as she forgave the man who disfigured her lovely face." Here is the account from

UP newsman Neal Corbett, as it appeared in newspapers throughout the country:

"I would think he must be suffering; anybody who's like that, we ought to feel sorry for him," said April Aaron of the man who had sent her to a hospital for three weeks, following a brutal San Francisco knife attack. April Aaron is a devout Mormon, 22 years of age... She is a secretary who's as pretty as her name, but her face has just one blemish— the right eye is missing. April lost it to the 'wildly slashing knife of a purse snatcher,' near San Francisco's Golden Gate Park while en route to a [youth] dance last April 18. She also suffered deep slashes on her left arm and right leg during a struggle with her assailant, after she tripped and fell in her efforts to elude him just one block from the Mormon chapel...

"I ran for a block and a half before he caught me. You can't run very fast on high heels," April said with a smile. Slashes on her leg were so severe doctors feared for a time it would need amputation. The sharp edge of the weapon could damage neither April's vivaciousness, nor her compassion. "I wish that somebody could do something for him to help him. He should have some treatment. Who knows what leads a person to do a thing like this? If they don't find him, he's likely to do it again."

...April Aaron has won the hearts of the people of San Francisco Bay area with her courage and good spirit in face of tragedy. Her room at St. Francis hospital was banked with flowers throughout her stay

and attendants said they couldn't recall when anyone received more cards and expressions of good wishes.

Modern psychology would probably dictate that April was simply repressing the horror of the attack, and that it would eventually catch up with her. But that is not the case. I met her for myself some years later. She was not April Aaron anymore, as she had married. She had a daughter the age of my younger children, and although I had read that account in "The Miracle of Forgiveness," I did not realize she was the woman from the story until later. All I saw was a pretty mom who was fun and had a beautiful family.

So, how is it that April was actually able to forgive this awful act that could have entirely ruined her life? I believe that only the Atonement of Jesus Christ has that kind of power. The kind where you can take something so terrible, and give it away. Drown it in the depths of the sea, where you remember it no more. And then take what you have been given, and make something truly beautiful.

It certainly makes you think about hurts and offenses of which you have not let go… why is it that in our human nature, and maybe more especially our *feminine* human nature, we find a perverse satisfaction in holding petty grudges and in feeling sorry for ourselves? I think that maybe it is because forgiveness requires faith… a leap we are sometimes unwilling or afraid to take. This thought really resonates with me: that forgiveness is *not an act of feelings, but one of will.* Can we *decide* to forgive?

One of my favorite scripture stories is that of the Prodigal Son. Very often we talk about the story of the prodigal son from the viewpoint of his brother. If you remember, the brother never went astray; he did not take his fortune from his father and go out and spend it and sow wild oats. He remained faithful and stayed and cared for his father's estate. He was naturally dismayed when the prodigal son returned and their father fell upon him, relieved and weeping, commanding that they should kill the fatted calf for a feast in his honor.

I, myself, have often related more to that brother. It seemed very unfair to make so much of the son who had fallen away and sinned. But there are many lessons to be learned from a parable. And for me, an important aspect of the Prodigal Son is to remember that no matter who we are, we are *all* that prodigal son. We have all strayed and fallen away, each in our own particular ways. We all depend on the Savior to atone for those sins. We are all beholden to Him for that grace, and we are all in need of that divine forgiveness.

The Lord wants us to forgive as we are forgiven; but not just for the person who has wronged us— even more for ourselves. Many years ago I had a close friend who was doing something that was hurting me. It was a persistent problem and at first I just ignored it, but my resentment built and built until one day it all came out in an explosion. Because I had been her friend for some time, and I knew exactly how to cut her with my words, I did just that. It felt so good— amazingly satisfying—for the space of about one minute. She had clearly been in the wrong and had been abusing my kindness and friendship; and when I called her out for all of it, I had my say and relieved all of my frustration with the situation. But almost immediately, and over the next many days, I was flooded with the realization that her actions had been born of unresolved traumas in her life— she had hurts of her own.

I did go back to my friend and ask her forgiveness. I knew that was something I had to do, and it wasn't a difficult thing. But what *was* difficult to do was the thing that would really change everything for me: I had to make that leap of faith and decide to forgive *her*.

I have always thought of forgiveness as being one of those principles that was easy for me. If someone asks for my forgiveness, I give it; immediately and wholeheartedly. Maybe I was even a little bit proud of that. But it is easier to grant forgiveness to someone who begs it; it is ever so much harder to give it freely when it is unasked. When I made the decision to humble myself and forgive my friend, I had such a feeling of relief. Peace instantly replaced all the conflict and unhappiness that had been brewing like a dark storm in my heart.

Heavenly Father wants us to forgive freely so that we can move on and be an instrument in his hands. He can't do anything with a person who is sitting around worrying about slights, and he can't do anything with one who never gets up from her knees praying for forgiveness. I love this scripture: Doctrine and Covenants 64:34. *Behold, the Lord requireth the heart and a willing mind.* Whatever hurt you have been harboring, now is the time to willingly give it up, so that the atonement of Jesus Christ can work miracles in your life. I love you!

The Lord is my shepherd; I shall not want. He maketh me to lie down in green pastures: he leadeth me beside the still waters…

Surely goodness and mercy shall follow me all the days of my life: and I will dwell in the house of the Lord for ever.

—Psalm 23

I had an experience last year that made me realize that goodness and mercy are following me; that testified to me of the love that God has for me.

I lost my keys, and they were missing for many months. I really hate losing things, and even had a tracker on the keyring, along with my house keys, mail key and car keys. I tried tracking them and the battery had run out on the tracker. It told me that they were last seen at my church. So for weeks, I looked everywhere at the church. I looked in my home and my car. I checked the "lost and found" at church week after week, and I had several friends also helping me look for the missing keys.

One friend who lived close by had a key to my house, and when she knew I was out, or visiting with family, she would use her key to let herself in and clean my house; vacuuming and scrubbing—and whenever she did, she would search under beds and furniture because she knew that I was missing those keys.

Nearly a year went by, and two local missionaries visited me because they wanted to record a video of my testimony, much like the reels I had been making for Off Her Rocker. We were in the family room trying to record that video, but my little dog, Lulu, kept making noises and distracting me as I was trying to speak.

So I asked one of the missionaries if he would take Lulu into my bedroom and close the door so that she wouldn't be in the video. He scooped her up and went into my bedroom and a few moments later I heard him quietly close the door and return. But to my utter amazement, he came back holding a large ring of keys—my missing keys! He said he walked into the bedroom and without even knowing why, he crossed the room to my tall dresser, stooped down, reached under it, and immediately laid his hand on this large ring of keys.

That was a miracle to me, but not just because I had my keys back. I had duplicates of all the keys, after all. I had completely given up on finding them after so long. But I also knew that I had searched under that dresser many times; in fact, several of us had, in the course of searching. But for them to be found, in that way, and at that exact time, when I was making a video to testify of Jesus Christ—that was the miracle I really needed. It felt like the Lord was telling me in a very personal way that I was doing the right thing. I am so grateful for this small miracle of God's love for me.

Chapter 12
Love and Breaking the Curve

"Neither do men light a candle, and put it under a bushel, but on a candlestick; and it giveth light unto all that are in the house. "Let your light so shine before men, that they may see your good works, and glorify your Father which is in heaven"
—Matthew 5:14–16

It took me many months in Lone Pine to recover from hepatitis. Many people who have that serious form of hepatitis have organ damage, and even if they recover, they are permanently weakened. My friend Barbara who had shared my convalescence only lived a few more years, into her thirties. I was most fortunate that I recovered entirely from that illness.

When I no longer had to be on bed rest, it was time to contact my mother and father in Las Vegas. I had to tell them that I had left my marriage; that I had been seriously ill. And I wanted to tell them that I finally had a plan.

I was going to take charge of my life and go back to college so that I could support myself and my children. By this time, my brother had also recovered sufficiently from his injuries that he was able to go back to his own place. So my dad drove out and picked up my little family, and we moved into their spare room there in Las Vegas, Nevada.

I shared with them my plan to go back to college and get a degree and a teaching certificate. When I asked them if I could stay with them while I did that, they readily agreed. My Aunt Chris and Uncle Earl visited during that time. They were rather well to do, and had no children of their own. They looked at my situation, and saw that I would be in school for the next four years, and they wanted to be helpful.

They bought me a little car so I would have transportation, and they paid for a small apartment with kitchen, bathroom and bedrooms to be added onto my parents' home for me to live in with my children for the duration of my university time. Aunt Chris was, in modern terms, a spicy character, and she had a tongue like one of our Death Valley scorpions. But she and Earl were angels on the earth for me as a young, single mother.

I was twenty-six years old, and I enrolled at University of Nevada, Las Vegas, (UNLV). I consulted with a counselor there, and we determined that it would take four years to graduate, and then about a year after that to earn my teaching certificate. But I was no longer the unmotivated seventeen-year-old who had dropped out of Chaffey College with failing grades. I was filled with determination, and I had done some very hard things. I knew that if I could do those hard things, I could certainly do more.

The school counselor recommended twelve credit hours per semester as a returning student. Fifteen would be considered a full course-load, and eighteen was the maximum recommended. Beyond that, I would have to petition the university to to allow me to take more. My first semester at UNLV, I took *twenty-five credit hours*. Some of those hours were classes I did not attend, but simply studied for, and challenged the final exam for full credit. I took twenty-two credit hours the second semester and then took every possible summer school class they offered. I did the same my second year, and I graduated in two years from UNLV.

There is a plot element in "Harry Potter and the Prisoner of Azkaban" by J.K. Rowling, in which Hermione Granger used a time-traveling medallion to jump back a few hours each day so that she could take more classes at Hogwarts. During those two years of university, I could have certainly have related to Hermione. My life was a blur of classes, homework, writing, studying and children. My parents cared for Greg and Shawn every day so that I could accomplish that feat.

In that flurry of academics, I learned not only all the subject matter I needed to become a teacher, but I also learned confidence. I think that in modern education, it is somewhat less common to "grade on a curve" but that was the primary grading model for all my classes in the 1950s.

In this particular model, the professor would look at all the test scores for a particular test. The highest score would set the curve, and all the other scores would be adjusted accordingly. This was generally beneficial to most of the students because if a test was very difficult and everyone scored rather low, all the scores would be adjusted up to reflect that. However, when everyone scores low, but one student scores very high, that person is considered to "break the curve."

For instance, if a test is very difficult and the average score is 60% but the highest score is 70%, the professor might opt to call that highest score 100%, and move up the score of everyone in the class by 30%, improving everyone's grades based on that high difficulty level. But if there is an outlier—a student who scores 96% when the average is 60%, then the grades may only be improved by 4%, leaving the bulk of the class in failure range, and that student essentially breaks the curve. When the same student consistently breaks the curve in all her classes, the other students can become, very understandably, antagonistic toward her… ask me how I know…

Well, you don't really need to ask. In my absolute determination to succeed in this second act of my college career, I broke most every curve during my two years. I also, again very understandably, did not make many friends during that time. I received a lot of pressure from other students to "dial it back;" to curb my academic enthusiasm.

But that was something I could not do, either for myself or my children. At the end of those two years, I received a letter from the governor of Nevada. It commended me for having the highest grade point average of any student in the whole University of Nevada system for those two years of college. I love this scripture in Matthew: 5:14 & 15: Ye are the light of the world. A city that is set on an hill cannot be hid. Neither do

men light a candle, and put it under a bushel, but on a candlestick; and it giveth light unto all that are in the house.

I often hear that scripture, as it relates to sharing one's testimony and faith. But I think it can also be aptly applied to dimming the light of our intellect and our gifts. Many times in my life, I have been told that I am too intense; intimidating; that I am trying too hard; breaking the curve. Especially as women, we are told to "sit still and look pretty." The world would tell us to dim our lights in order to make others more comfortable.

For most of my life up to that point, I did not want people to look at me. I was the small, scar-faced girl hiding in my mother's closet. I was the shy debutante who didn't know how to talk to my peers. I was the girl who did laundry and kept house for a cheating husband.

I was finished being that girl—any of those girls—and I would not, *could not,* be the girl who "dumbed down" her tests to make classmates happy. Rather, I was the woman who let her light shine for herself and her children.

You have gifts and a light within you that is unique in all the world. You cannot, for anyone, dim that light simply to make them more comfortable. You have those around you who can only grow and thrive when they bask in your beautiful golden light.

As your light grows strong enough, you can be like a beacon in a lighthouse that shines much, much further, cutting through the blackest nights and the most turbulent storms, to guide those who have wandered far.

You may never even know how far you cast your light, or all those that you may touch. I pray that you grow in love and confidence until you are truly luminous. I promise you that is how your Heavenly Father sees you. I love you!

Judge not that you be not judged.
— Matthew 7:1

One day I was in the grocery store and I came across one of our neighbor boys, Mark, whom I thought of as the terror of the neighborhood. He wasn't more than ten years old, and he had a list of offenses that was a mile long, including setting fire to a neighbor's garage, breaking into homes and stealing, and spray-painting another neighbor's car. I thought to myself that he needed to be disciplined and that his parents were obviously doing a poor job.

On this day, as I pushed my cart I rounded a corner into the aisle that sold baby items. Mark was crouched in front of a display of baby food and was methodically opening each jar to hear the pop of the vacuum seal releasing. I didn't say anything to him, but found his mother in an adjacent aisle and alerted her to his infraction.

She shrugged miserably and then hurried to the baby aisle. I tagged along to see if she needed any help. Mark's mother yelled at him and called him stupid and slapped his face several times.

I had not improved the situation by pointing out his errors to his mother. Her actions were born of frustration and desperation, and I can still see the whipped, defeated look on young Mark's red face. I have thought since then that what he needed was someone to sit down beside him to talk to him and to listen to him; to let him know he was okay. His mother needed the same thing, not my judgment of her parenting. I believe that deep down, that is what each of us needs, most all the time.

How much happier would our lives be, if, each day, we prayed to know how we can best help others? Who can we sit down with, without judgment; talk to them, listen, and let them know that they are okay?

Chapter 13
Love and a Changed Heart

I have told you that in my childhood, I felt a warm connection to God, even though my family was not particularly religious. I read the New Testament, unbidden, and I prayed and felt that my prayers were answered. I had what I would call spiritual experiences, and these experiences for a small girl rambling in the desert, were a beautiful gift. As such, you would think they would be the foundation for feeling closer and closer to God as I grew up.

But sadly, that is not the way spiritual experiences, or a testimony of God actually works, is it? There is something in our human makeup that allows us to put those feelings and experiences away from us as we grow. A feeling of joy and love flooding into one's heart as an eight-year-old, even *knowing* at that time that it came from God— can be brushed off as nothing by a stubborn teenager who only thinks about boys, or school, or about how she is perceived by others.

I often think of a line from Charles Dickens' "A Christmas Carol, when Ebenezer Scrooge was confronted by the ghost of his old partner, the long-dead Jacob Marley. Ebenezer was an old man with a cold, hard heart, and even in the face of a *literal* spiritual experience, he tried to explain it away by saying, "You may be an undigested bit of beef, a blot of mustard, a crumb of cheese, a fragment of underdone potato. There's more of gravy than of grave about you, whatever you are!"

I believe that on most occasions, the Spirit of God whispers to us, and the world—well, it is very loud. So it was that I grew from a spiritual child to be a lone pine as those childhood days faded away. Putting away those lone pine days meant much more than moving home with my parents and accepting help as I recovered from illness. In fact, it would require a change of heart and fresh eyes and ears so that I could once again hear the whisperings of the Spirit and see God's hand in my life. I would need to be spiritually born again.

As I finished my university degree and prepared to pursue my teaching certificate, I began filling out job applications for teaching jobs. This was a wonderfully exciting era of my life. I finally felt, at the age of 28, that I had my life on a good track for myself and my two children. The thought of living on my own and working as a school teacher, without the countless hours of study and homework was a dream, come true.

I was sitting in the library at the university of Nevada when a man I had shared classes with, came up to me at a research desk. He handed me an application to teach school in Caliente, Nevada. I had before me three applications: Las Vegas, Nevada, Lone Pine, California, and a ghost town near Goldfield, Nevada. I had mostly chosen those locations because I knew people there. I remember him saying, "You need to apply to teach in Caliente, Nevada," and I thought to myself that I knew no one there; I had no reason to do so— but I added it to my pile and filled it out because it was there.

When the offers of employment started coming back, I had offers from all four schools. Las Vegas was the best money and I would be near my parents; I could see how that would be good for my children. Of all the schools, Caliente was the poorest paying, by quite a lot. There was nothing enticing about it. I didn't know much about it, and what I could find when I looked it up, did not recommend it. But as soon as I started looking at those letters, I absolutely knew that I would be going to Caliente, Nevada. This knowledge came to me as a feeling, one of those whisperings of the Spirit. Against outward appearances to the contrary, this choice just felt right.

That was an exhilarating time as I prepared to go to Caliente. My parents were quite happy about it and encouraging. They took me there prior to the school year. Again, Caliente was not particularly attractive. It had been a big railroad terminal from Las Vegas and the railroads had routed a lot of repairs and shipping through there, but when the bulk of that business shifted to Las Vegas, Caliente became almost a ghost town.

I really enjoyed getting my clothes ready; my kids prepared. With the help of the school principal's wife I found a little place to rent. It was a separate little home in the backyard of the home of a family there. Greg was seven years old and would attend the elementary school where I taught that year, but Shawn was in kindergarten which was only a half day, so the woman who rented me that small house agreed to provide childcare for Shawn each day when she got out of kindergarten.

The school principal's wife was very kind, and during my first week of school, she invited me to a potluck dinner at her church. I had only been in Caliente a very few days, and I didn't know anyone outside of school. They had wonderful food and were so welcoming. I suddenly realized that Shawn was not there. I desperately looked around, and the principal's wife helped me. She alerted the other church members and almost instantly the entire group was all out looking for Shawn.

A couple found her walking down the streets of Caliente, quite a way from the church, and she was very calm. She said she had decided she wanted to go home from the potluck, so without telling me or anyone else, she had just started walking.

I felt as though my heart was in my throat every moment that Shawn was missing, but it was new and very comforting to find that I had a community of people who cared about me, and it made me think about attending church meetings with my children.

A couple that were parents of one of my students came in after school one day, and they told me they were missionaries from the Church of Jesus Christ of Latter-Day Saints, and they asked if I was interested in learning more about Jesus Christ. I found that for maybe the first time in my life, I was totally open to that.

I had never had any religious affiliation up to that point. When I was a fourteen-year-old at Duffy Girls' School, I had a drivers license. I have to pause at this point to tell you that I had no business driving at that age; once a year an inspector from the DMV in Independence, California drove out to Death Valley to provide motor vehicle and licensing services for people in the area. That summer when I had just turned fourteen, he was there and he turned to my dad and asked, "How old is Kay?" indicating me. My dad told him I was fourteen, and he said, "Well, why don't I go ahead and give her a license while I'm here?" and proceeded to fill out the license for me, without any kind of testing or driving experience.

While I attended Duffy Girls' School, even though I was a very inexperienced and timid driver, the administrator there was relieved to have someone else who could drive. So every Sunday she handed me the keys to the school station wagon and instructed me to take all the girls to their various churches in town.

Church services were a new experience for me, so I attended quite a number of churches during those last two years of my high school. I had never really felt touched by any of them, but at the time when the couple asked if I would like to have lessons about Jesus Christ, and about their church, I felt once again that same confirming spirit that "Yes, this is what you should do." So I happily said yes.

They had several lessons, and after the first lesson about God, the Father and Jesus Christ, they gave me some scriptures to read before we met again the following week. But I found myself thirsting for this word of God, and I read everything in one week. All the scriptures and everything I could get my hands on. They were so surprised when we met again, and started teaching me the lessons at a faster pace.

I had so many questions for them. I was amazed because any church I had been to before, never seemed to have answers to my questions. Instead they had excuses. So I was surprised and excited that they knew the answers to "Where did i come from?" and "Why am i here?" and "Where am i going?" The answers made so much sense to me and they just felt right. By our fourth meeting together, I told them that I wanted to be baptized.

During those first months in Caliente, I would teach my class of second graders Monday through Friday, and then Greg, Shawn and I would pack a few things and drive about an hour to my parents' home in Las Vegas to spend the weekend with them. I told my parents that I wanted to be baptized. I was 28 years old and didn't need permission, but I was old enough to appreciate their counsel instead of thinking I wanted and needed to do everything myself.

My mother told me that it was okay if I wanted to be baptized in the Mormon church, but they were asking me to wait one year. Mother told me that everything I did, I did with great intensity. When she said that, it was an interesting thought to me. Many people had told me in my life that I was way too intense. I never liked when they would say that, because most often they were people who wanted me to excuse their bad behavior or lack of motivation.

I think it is important to be intense with things that are important. But coming from my gentle and thoughtful mother, I knew that what she said made sense. I could wait a year; go to church and study, but wait to be baptized until that first intensity lessened. Maybe my parents thought I would change my mind in that time.

I did not change my mind. But that year changed my heart. I had lived close to three decades learning, growing and making mistakes. But something happened when I was attending church and preparing to be baptized. For the first time since I was a child, I was allowing the things I learned to actually touch my heart and to change it.

All my intensity up to that point had been a way of controlling my life; a way of taking charge and making my own way. And those were good things, mostly. But what God requires of us is "the heart and a willing mind," as it says in D&C: 64:34. Instead of taking charge and making things go exactly how I planned, I was learning to give myself to Him; I was ready to see what he could make of me. It took a great deal of faith to do that, and I was developing that faith.

In "The Silver Chair," part of the Chronicles of Narnia by C.S. Lewis, Jill Pole was new to Narnia, and she had an allegorical exchange with the great lion, Aslan. Jill was terribly thirsty and to her relief she found a stream in the woods, but there was an enormous lion sitting on the ground between her and the object of her desire. Aslan told her to come and have a drink, but instead she asked him to move away. At this request, Aslan growled. They were his waters, and she was invited to drink, but not on her terms.

Jill wanted reassurance, so she asked Aslan if he eats little girls. His reply truly terrified her: "I have swallowed up girls and boys, women and men, kings and emperors, cities and realms." Upon hearing this, Jill told Aslan that she dared not come closer and drink, but Aslan gently reminded her that in that case she would simply die of thirst.

I could relate to Jill. I wanted blessings from God, but I wanted them on my own terms. I wanted to do everything my own way, but still drink from those living waters. When I humbled myself and had the faith to submit to God's will for me, only then could I drink; only then could my heart truly change.

That year I went from Caliente, Nevada to summer school in Reno to finish my teaching certificate, and for the following fall I would not return to Caliente, but instead would spend my second year teaching in Lone Pine, California. My summer in Reno was lonely and although I attended church services, the congregation was not welcoming. I scarcely talked to another soul there, and no one really tried to talk to me. I nurtured my fledgling faith through study and reading the scriptures that summer.

But in the fall, the small town of Lone Pine came through for me again. The very first time I attended the tiny church there—a small congregation of no more than forty or fifty—I believe I was hugged by every person. I had never been in any place where I felt more loved; for that reason it was a wonderful year for me.

In October, my year spent waiting to be baptized was complete, and I contacted those sweet missionaries from Caliente. They had taught me so much, and we had grown close. Their names were Skeet and Mary. Skeet had his own airplane, so they flew from Caliente to Lone Pine, and I was baptized.

Being baptized— taking the name of Jesus Christ and being numbered one of His own, is one of the singular experiences of my life. It was one of those "before and after" events. There is *before I was baptized,* and *after*. I found that "after" was my happy place. I was baptized on a Saturday, and on Monday I stood in the schoolyard sunshine watching after the elementary school students during recess. I felt this glow well up within my changed heart.

The thought came to me out on that playground: "I will never have to have another worry, because my faith in Jesus Christ will conquer everything." I came to realize how unrealistic that thought was, because that is not how faith or life works. We will always have afflictions and learn to grow through them.

But the glow in my heart was absolutely real; it was a burgeoning testimony in Jesus Christ and I have felt it warm me many times since— in all the lovely times as well as in all the difficult times. It was not just a good feeling; it was a call to action. I wanted to help others around me and I wanted to be Christlike. I wanted to be more. I wanted to be better. Even now, as I near the end of my time on this earth, I still feel that glow inside me, and despite my weakened condition, I am still moved to do the best I can with this time I have.

In 1 Corinthians 5:17 it says: "Therefore if any man be in Christ, he is a new creature." I was indeed a new creature, and I looked at those around me differently. Teaching second grade was probably my favorite of all the years that I taught. The kids that age are still more oriented toward the teacher than to their peers, and I was teaching them very exciting things.

I remember looking at a group of kindergartners that year, and thinking what perfect, precious little humans they were. By the following June, they would leave school for the summer and some of them would feel after that school year that they were loved and smart and appreciated. Others would go home for the summer knowing that they were not loved; that they were not smart enough to learn what they were supposed to.

It crushed me to think that any child would feel the latter. If it was in my power to help the kids I taught to feel loved and successful, then I would do that. It wasn't that I had not wanted to be a good teacher before I was baptized; it was just that I felt a newfound responsibility to care for others if I could.

There is a poem by Leigh Hunt that I memorized many years ago, and I want to share it with you because it has a beautiful lesson in it.

Abou Ben Adhem
Abou Ben Adhem (may his tribe increase!)
Awoke one night from a deep dream of peace,
And saw, within the moonlight in his room,
Making it rich, and like a lily in bloom,
An angel writing in a book of gold:—
Exceeding peace had made Ben Adhem bold,
And to the presence in the room he said,
"What writest thou?"—The vision raised its head,
And with a look made of all sweet accord,
Answered, "The names of those who love the Lord."
"And is mine one?" said Abou. "Nay, not so,"
Replied the angel. Abou spoke more low,
But cheerly still; and said, "I pray thee, then,
Write me as one that loves his fellow men."

The angel wrote, and vanished. The next night
It came again with a great wakening light,
And showed the names whom love of God had blest,
And lo! Ben Adhem's name led all the rest.

Remember I told you in the very introduction of the book, I have learned that the most important thing is always love. I am grateful every day of my life for the experiences that led me to learn about my Savior Jesus Christ. I am grateful for my changed heart and that I am baptized in his holy name. I am grateful for that glow that warms me like schoolyard sunshine even today. And I love you!

Chapter 14
Love and the Hero in My Story

Invictus
Out of the night that covers me,
Black as the pit from pole to pole,
I thank whatever gods may be
For my unconquerable soul.
In the fell clutch of circumstance
I have not winced nor cried aloud.
Under the bludgeonings of chance
My head is bloody, but unbowed.
Beyond this place of wrath and tears
Looms but the Horror of the shade,
And yet the menace of the years
Finds and shall find me unafraid.
It matters not how strait the gate,
How charged with punishments the scroll,
I am the master of my fate,
I am the captain of my soul.
—William Ernest Henley

God has commanded us to love our neighbors as ourselves. It is important to look at that commandment and see that God expects us to actually *love ourselves.* It has taken me a lifetime to first realize that, and then to work toward making it happen. I don't think I am alone in this struggle. Even people who seem to only care about themselves often are masking the fact that they don't love themselves at all.

Self-care and self-love have become catchphrases that we hear quite a lot, and they can sometimes be used to excuse selfishness and bad behavior. Sometimes the phrase "self care" conjures ideas of manicures and decadent food. But it is much more than that.

Leaving catchphrases aside, I believe that learning to love ourselves is something we have to do before we can truly be Christlike and love others. I find it helpful to remind myself regularly that I am a child of God; that he loves me and sees the best in me; and that I should do the same. But merely knowing that is not always enough.

You may not think much about whether you love yourself, but I find for myself that when I am falling down in this area, there are symptoms ranging from debilitating worry to problems sleeping. You may notice signs when you are not taking care of yourself. I would like to focus on three of these things because for me, they are most telling, and because they are things I can work on to make a great positive impact on my wellbeing.

Have you ever caught sight of yourself as you walk past a mirror, or maybe spotted yourself in a candid photograph, and notice that you are slouching when you walk, or sliding down in a chair when you sit? Posture is a huge indicator for me of whether I am happy with myself. Poor posture is a way of shrinking in on myself, and trying to be invisible.

Another example of this is walking into a church meeting and looking for a seat way in the back where I won't be observed or asked to participate. This is such an easy fix, and the amazing thing is that changing to a straight, confident posture not only changes how others see you, but it almost instantly changes your outlook and how you see yourself.

The second thing is an internal symptom that has the most devastating effect on my self-image. It is something I will simply call negative conversation. I am sure I am not the only one who has conversations with myself on a regular basis. It probably happens more now that I am old as dirt, without a lot of young people to look after. But even when I was a mother of six at home, I sabotaged myself with negative conversations.

These negative conversations could be as simple as lying awake at night thinking about how I had failed to make dental appointments for my kids and now they were overdue and would certainly all have cavities. They could be very serious conversations in which I continued to punish myself for a transgression; one for which I had previously repented and been forgiven. I might even think about how I had been treated badly by someone and all the reasons why it was actually my fault.

These negative conversations can be so destructive. The best way to combat them is first, to recognize them; to see them for for what they are and admit that they are harmful. Then I like to imagine having those same conversations with a loved one. Would I ever say those things to someone I love? Would I accuse them and blame them and try to make them feel unlovable? Of course not! I would not crush someone in that way. So why do I feel that it is okay to speak to myself in that manner?

A few years ago I was sitting in church, and a young woman in her thirties was giving a talk from the pulpit. She was new to the congregation and I didn't know her, or even much about her. My mind wandered from her topic, and I found myself thinking that the dress she was wearing was very unbecoming. It was too tight across the chest and was cutting into her upper arms. She knew she was to speak in church that day, and yet her hair looked like it was still wet. She sounded nervous and she was telling a story about reading scriptures. I was pretty sure she didn't have anything to teach me on that topic that I didn't already know.

All of those observations took place in the space of twenty or thirty seconds. She was judged and found wanting, and I didn't even know her. This sounds petty and judgmental—and it is; but it is also human nature to observe and judge. I have a thought exercise that I do to combat this undesirable human pettiness.

I looked at her again, and this time I thought of her as my little sister. I imagined that she was my little sister whom I loved. I was her biggest cheerleader. I knew that she was absolutely trying her best, and I began to pray in my mind that she would do a good job speaking. I prayed that she would feel strong and uplifted. I prayed that I would learn something from her talk.

I opened my eyes and looked up at her again and found that she had changed in the time it took me to pray. She had managed to fit into her prettiest dress, even though I noticed that her eyes kept going to her husband in one of the front rows. He was holding their new baby. How stressful it must have been preparing for that talk when she had a newborn to care for—her first. I later became well-acquainted with this young woman, and felt fortunate to know her. She was a gifted teacher, and a beautiful mother who lost her own parents when she was young.

I am grateful that I was able to put aside judgment and see her for the divine daughter of God that she is. It is a harder thing to apply that same grace to myself; to see myself for the divine, gifted daughter of God that I am. But it is worth the effort. I am worth the effort.

The third sign that I notice when I am not taking proper care of myself is a very obvious one—it is simply that I am not physically taking care. This encompasses everything from eating healthy foods, to hygiene, to making an effort with my physical appearance. It is not vain to try to look nice and make healthy choices. Our Heavenly Father has given us these mortal bodies, and it is our sacred responsibility to care for them.

For a few decades, I only wore black. The black had a dual purpose: the first was that I imagined it made me look skinnier, and secondly it was camoflauge; armor even. I thought it granted me some sort of invisibility; protection from the eyes of others. Truthfully, it was probably ineffective at all those things. The woman at the 4th of July picnic shrouded in head-to-toe black doesn't exactly blend in, does she? Wearing all black was just part of trying to hide my physical appearance, rather than caring for it.

Once I learned to recognize the symptoms of my lack of self-love, not only was I able to address them and care for myself the way I should, but I was also able to see those symptoms in others. When I notice that my best friend has not washed her hair in two weeks, and that she is wearing the same pajama pants that she was two days ago, I don't think to myself that she is disgusting and unclean. Rather, I realize that she is feeling unlovable—not even worthy of her *own* love. She needs to lean on the love that I have for her.

In the later days of my first marriage to Buck, I was miserably unhappy. It was understandable, since I had two small children and my husband was seeing other women. We were living in a little town right outside of Yosemite, and I felt isolated and lonely. One day my friend Miriam from the Big Trees Resort came to see me.

I looked rundown and awful, and felt very sorry for myself. I poured out all of my frustration and heartache to Miriam. My friend listened to me for a few minutes, then she came over and sat in front of me and held both my hands. She said, "I'm going to teach you a life skill."

"I want you to think of one thing that brings you a little bit of pleasure," she said. I thought she was trying to cheer me up and I wasn't having any of it. I replied that there wasn't anything. My life was simply terrible. But Miriam patiently asked me, "Do you enjoy a cup of coffee in the morning?" I agreed that I did. "You see," she said, "That brings you a little bit of pleasure."

At that point I got up and made two cups of coffee, and we sipped and talked. And I realized that while she was there and I was drinking that cup of coffee, that I didn't hurt so much. After we finished our coffee, she told me that I had to think of other things that brought me a little bit of happiness. "Every day…" she instructed me. "Every day you have to think of a few things that bring you a little bit of pleasure, no matter how small. After a time, you will find out that you can control, to a degree, that misery that you are feeling."

That day, Marion truly taught me a lesson in self-care. I didn't forget the lesson, either. Each day I thought of some very small things that were just for me. I made myself a priority for those very few minutes a day. It didn't make my troubles go away, but it was a reminder to myself that I was worthy of love and care, and that helped me push through the hard times that were to come.

Before I close this chapter, I want to draw your attention back to the poem at the beginning. I memorized Invictus when I was quite young, but I don't think I really appreciated it until I was much older. I absolutely love each line. I *have* done hard things and stayed strong.

Now when I read it, I envision myself in each line. When I was young, I felt like I was playing a bit part in the play of my life. I worked my way up to sidekick, then main character. And now I see, after all this time, how I have been the hero in my story all along, even when I made mistakes. Don't take too long to realize this about yourself. *You are the hero in your story.* Stand up straight. Wear something light blue. Do hard things and love yourself even when you fall short. I love you!

"My grace is sufficient for thee: for my strength is made perfect in weakness."
—2 Corinthians 12:9

When my youngest daughter, Wendy, was small, she was painfully shy. She was so bright and gifted and caring of others, that I always prayed she could overcome her shyness so that people could see what a wonderful girl she was.

She did overcome the shyness, and kept all the great qualities. She became a talented musician and a great student, and beloved by her many friends. I still thought of her as being somewhat reserved. When she was 21, she decided to serve a church mission and she went to West Germany for a year and a half.

Shortly after she returned, she and I went to the grocery store to pick up a few items, and went to the front of the store to make our purchases. There were a few people in line ahead of us, so we waited there with our cart.

Before I even realized who she was talking to, Wendy turned around in the line and struck up a conversation with the woman resting against her shopping cart behind us. Without much small talk, I heard her ask the woman if she knew about Jesus Christ.

I don't recall the woman's response, or if anything came of that conversation. But the experience was a testament to me that God can take our weaknesses and turn them into strengths. I was in awe of the quiet and warm-hearted way that Wendy could speak of Jesus Christ and bear testimony of Him, even to a stranger in a grocery store.

Chapter 15
Love and the Back Fence

God's World
O world, I cannot hold thee close enough!
Thy winds, thy wide grey skies!
Thy mists, that roll and rise!
Thy woods, this autumn day, that ache and sag
And all but cry with colour! That gaunt crag
To crush! To lift the lean of that black bluff!
World, World, I cannot get thee close enough!

Long have I known a glory in it all,
But never knew I this;
Here such a passion is
As stretcheth me apart, — Lord, I do fear
Thou'st made the world too beautiful this year;
My soul is all but out of me, — let fall
No burning leaf; prithee, let no bird call.
— Edna St. Vincent Millay

In the beginning, God created the heaven and the earth. And oh, what a beautiful earth it is! I cannot share the things that make me happy in this life without talking about nature.

I think that one of the things that really connected me with Parley is that the outdoors and its beauty were so important to him. In the last ten years of his life, we lived in Southern Oregon. He was retired from working in the glass business.

I know a lot of people think that retirement will be so great; that they will finally have time to enjoy life. And then when they actually retire, they find that they are bored, and not quite sure what to do with all that free time. That was never Parley. He always had projects and interests and things to work on. But I have never met anyone who was so good at just having fun.

Parley would make us pancakes for breakfast and then say, "Let's go for a drive." He would throw a big mattress into the pickup bed, call our two golden retrievers, and we would drive a short distance down into California to the Klamath River. We would spend a lovely evening in the green woods, throwing sticks for the dogs and wading in the river. We would eat a simple dinner and then sleep in the bed of the truck under a lush canopy of stars.

When thru the woods and
forest glades I wander,
And hear the birds sing
sweetly in the trees,
When I look down from
lofty mountain grandeur
And hear the brook and feel
the gentle breeze
Then sings my soul, my
Savior God, to thee,
How great thou art! How
great thou art!
—Stuart K. Hine

I haven't had Parley for many years, and I thought that my days of exploring were over. I remember feeling when I was young that I had the vast, wide earth to explore and sometimes it was like lightning in my veins. I could climb to the top of Black Butte in a morning and from there, look out at snowcapped Mt. Shasta, so close I imagined I could reach out and touch it. But as I began grew older, my vision began to cloud. I could not simply drive wherever I wanted. I could not walk as far as I used to. It seemed like my world was becoming smaller, and would only grow smaller still with the passing of each day.

However, my children and grandchildren began to take me on lovely adventures. I am blessed to live in a wonderland of forests, lakes and ocean within short driving distances. One of my daughters told me that she knew it was what her dad would have wanted, and she is right. Being in the outdoors meant so much to Parley. With every trip to Crater Lake or Dead Indian Loop, or further afield to visit my beloved Death Valley, my world opened back up and felt vast and majestic again.

Once this past fall, I had been feeling like my world was shrinking, as it filled with nurses' visits and shortness of breath and very little adventure. At about 4:00 p.m., as I was thinking about a nap, my daughter and I suddenly had the idea of a drive. The destination I had in mind was Beckie's— a little cafe that's been around since the 1920s; specialty of the house: pie.

It was an hour and a half away up in the mountains next to the Rogue River Gorge, and it closed at 6:00 pm. We would just make it.

The food was lovely. There was clam chowder and cherry pie. The small log cabin that housed the landmark diner was cozy and smelled slightly of woodsmoke. The best part, though, was the view out the window that was like some kind of liniment for my sore body.

After our early dinner, I figured we had better get home, because the elevation was making me a little breathless, but it was twenty-five minutes to sunset and we were twenty-five miles from Crater Lake. I decided we were going for it. We got there after the sun had already set, but there was still enough gold spilling over the mountain to light that incredible lake on fire. My heart was ready to get back to the lower elevation, but my world had opened up again.

My health has not allowed even for mini-adventures for some months now, but I do not mourn this loss. I have laid away a treasure trove of memories —memories of all the beautiful places; all the lovely

experiences. I can imagine that wherever you live, while the scenery may be quite different, the love of the land is the same. I could never show you all the places that hold an eternal place in my heart, but I hope that the reverence for these places shines through. Two years ago, I went on a trip through many of the western states. On the way back we took a few hours' detour in order to visit Parley's grave. I had many memories of the high mountain town where he grew up. We had visited many times for family reunions. I remembered it as a beautiful little town with lightning storms that would roll in every summer afternoon to turn the sky orange and quench the thirsty trees and flowers and bring the neighborhood children in for snacks and naps. I remembered the spare landscape in the 6800-foot elevation as we would approach the town, but also how that stark beauty would give way to lovingly kept yards full of flowers and green grass.

On this particular summer afternoon, we drove into the town and found street after street of unkempt dirt yards, often littered with ancient appliances. We found some of the tiny historical homes, including one where my husband was born, collapsed in the tall, unkempt vegetation. Saddest of all, to me at least—there was not a single flower to be seen.

I know I am old-fashioned, but it is important to me to plant flowers. Making my yard a lovely haven matters to me. In these days when I can no longer explore further than my own backyard, I am not dismayed, because I am still in the beauty of the outdoors. I pass at least an hour or two there most days. I sit under giant sheltering maple trees, listening to the music of wind chimes and enjoying my flower beds, fall leaves and the occasional deer stopping by for a meal.

"Who has not felt the urge to throw a loaf of bread and a pound of tea in an old sack and jump over the back fence?"

—John Muir

I have been looking rather longingly at that back fence lately. My days of jumping over it are past, but I find so much natural beauty on my side of the fence. When I know that I can't venture far, I can take a deep breath and find the beauty right where I stand. Each season brings new wonders to my very own back yard.

Wherever you are—whatever it looks like there, I hope you find yourself outdoors often. And even if you can't venture far, you can still improve your little corner of the world. I hope you will plant some flowers for me; how I do love flowers! I love you.

"Wherefore, ye must press forward with a steadfastness in Christ, having a perfect brightness of hope, and a love of God and of all men."
—2 Nephi 31:20

I love the thought of pressing forward with a *perfect brightness of hope.* Hope is such an important principle to keep us focused on our purpose here on earth. One night I walked a short way down my street to my mailbox in the dark. I had a flashlight, but it grew more dim with each step. Its dim little beam lasted the fifty yards to the mailbox, but the batteries gave out entirely halfway back.

I was close to my house and not worried about making it back, but the darkness pressed in and I felt myself opening my eyes very wide as if trying to extract any little bit of light from it that I could. I reached the edge of my property and I miscalculated the step up onto the sidewalk.

Letters flew out of my hands and I heard the flashlight hit the curb. The dark was so disorienting that I wasn't able to even try to catch myself to break my fall, and it felt as though I skidded a couple of feet, leaving me bruised and skinned.

My eyes stung as I just laid there for a few seconds, taking stock of the damage to my knees, hands and arms. I was sore for a couple days after, but thankfully there were no serious injuries. I thought of the phrase "Everything stops bleeding eventually."

There have been times in my life when my hope has dimmed very much like that flashlight that I recovered from the gutter the next morning. Our hope is what allows us to see a way forward. Hope is happiness. More than two centuries ago, Henry Francis Lyte wrote the text to one of my favorite hymns, "Abide With Me." The first verse speaks so clearly of our human plight:

Abide with me: fast falls the eventide;
the darkness deepens; Lord, with me abide.
When other helpers fail and comforts flee,
Help of the helpless, O abide with me.

Without the hope that we feel, through our Savior, Jesus Christ, this life's day would seem dark, indeed, but that hope makes even the unbearable things, bearable. One way I express my hope in Jesus Christ is by making my reels on Instagram. It is that perfect brightness of hope; that love of God and of all men and women, that gives me strength to share my testimony with those around me and to expand my reach in ways I could never have imagined. That hope has blessed me beyond measure. I find that the more I share, the more I have. I love you!

Chapter 16
Love and a Phonograph

I met my beloved Parley when I was about 30 years old. I walked into a church service in Mt. Shasta, California with my two children. Parley was sitting at the front, as he was one of the counselors to the leader of that branch. He told me later that he knew, the instant he saw me, that I was "the one" for him. I don't know if that was exactly the case, but I definitely did draw attention that day.

I settled into one of the benches with Greg and Shawn. I was a school teacher there in that small town, and as I was in charge of the playground during recesses, I had taken to wearing a large silver whistle on a long chain around my neck. Even though it was Sunday, I had pulled the whistle over my head that morning and let it drop down like a necklace over my sheath dress. Twenty minutes into the church meeting, during a reverent, silent sacrament service, eight-year-old Greg blew that whistle, long and loudly. I never liked all eyes on me, so that was a startling moment for everyone.

I got to know Parley gradually over the course of a year. I had never met anyone like him. Up to that point in my life, I had loved people, and especially in the case of my children, I tried to tell them that and to show them. But when it came to expressing it, my love was a small, lukewarm stream of water from the bathroom sink. Parley's love for people was like a hot, invigorating shower.

It was a puzzle for me at first, figuring out what to do with this huge man with a booming voice and a smart, wicked sense of humor who made everyone feel like they were his very best friend. I was a single mother; a school teacher living in a small town. I had already experienced being with someone popular who had a big personality, and I felt like I had been swallowed up in that; chewed up and spit out at the side of the highway, much worse for the wear. I did not plan to marry again, and certainly not to someone who seemed so entirely foreign to my reserved demeanor.

For about a year, I observed Parley and got to know him. He was in the leadership of the local church. He had a daughter from his first marriage who was beautiful, getting straight A's in school, and always was so good and kind that I wanted her to spend time around my kids so those wonderful qualities would rub off on them. He loved the outdoors, his family, and people in general.

I taught school that year in Mt. Shasta, California and as the school year came to a close, the school board told me that they wanted me to stay in the school district, but that what they really needed was someone who could teach the special education class. They wanted me to return to Las Vegas and receive training over the summer, and then return to teach in the neighboring town of Fort Jones in the fall.

I moved out to Fort Jones at the end of that summer. It was a very rural place, and the home that I found to rent was a small, cozy house built on a huge cattle ranch there. Fort Jones got a lot of snow in the winter and the home, like most of that time, was heated by a wood stove. As soon as I rented that house and moved in, Parley started bringing me fuel for that stove.

The first weekend, Parley drove out in his pickup truck, and the truck bed was full of large rounds he had cut from a huge tree trunk. Each one probably weighed sixty pounds, and one by one he took them from the truck bed and split each one into several pieces of firewood of varying sizes. It took most of the day to split and chop all that wood, and I stayed out there with him, talking to him and then carrying the firewood to a shelter along the side of the house where it could be stacked and stored up for the winter.

I found that for the first time in my life, Parley was a man that I truly wanted to talk to. We talked nonstop, about everything under the sun. And as the sun began to set and he split the last log into small kindling that would make it easy to start my fires, I did not want to see him finish and go. Parley told me he had one last thing for me. The bed of the pickup was completely empty by then, and I could not imagine what else there could be.

Parley walked around to the passenger door of the truck and lifted out a large phonograph and carried it up the steps to my house and set it up in the living room. Then he went back out to the pickup and carried in a tall stack of vinyl records in their sleeves. I had spoken enough with Parley by then— both that day, and over the previous year— to know that for him, music was one of the most important things; particularly, classical music.

I was the recipient, all that day, of his great act of service. The phonograph was a particular sort of love language, though. It was his personal record player, and all of his favorite music, and he wanted to me to have that in my home so that I could be surrounded by beautiful music all the time.

That day marked a lot of things. It was the day I knew Parley loved me, and that I loved him back. It was the day I realized I wanted to be married again, to the right person. But it was also my first "love lesson." Parley didn't set out to teach me lessons, but by example, he constantly taught love lessons. I learned these lessons over the next forty years and I suppose that, given the fact that I am even writing this, I am still learning Parley's love lessons.

Parley did not love reservedly, or mildly. He did not refrain from expressing his love to anyone, whether they were family, friends, or even perfect strangers. He did not withhold praise and he was never stingy with admiration or appreciation.

Of course, Parley was not perfect. Neither was I. In those early years of our marriage, blending two young families together, loving was not always easy. We were not always kind, nor did we always hold our tempers.

Shortly after we were married, Parley got a call from his first wife, about their daughter, Lynne. Lynne had been living mostly with her grandparents; Parley's parents, out on their ranch in Northern California. Her mother did not feel capable of keeping her full time, and felt most comfortable, prior to our marriage, with Parley's parents at Hillcrest Orchards. When she called, it was to schedule a lunch, not with Parley, but with me. I was very interested to find out what the lunch was about, and I met her at Olive Garden in Redding one Saturday.

That lunch was a very interesting one. I very much liked Parley's ex-wife. She had so many questions for me that it almost seemed like a job interview. It turned out that it was, in a way. She wanted to know about my kids; about how we all got along; about what we did for discipline; cooking and mealtimes. She wanted to know all about our family, and at the end of the lunch, she told me that she was going to grant us full custody of Lynne, which was something I very much wanted.

Lynne and my daughter Shawn were close in age and good friends, and they always seemed to take good care of each other. That was something that always pleased me. Lynne was wonderful and so easy to love, and from then on, she was as much my daughter as Shawn was.

I told a story on instagram from this time in our lives. Parley loved everyone, but at this time of our family life, and particularly to my kids from my previous marriage, he was a big bear of a man; intimidating, and rather strict. We had, by that time, the three teenagers, along with three little ones who had been born over the first five years of our marriage.

On that particular day, Parley and I had left the three youngest in the care of the teenagers, and we were going up to the mountain to cut some firewood. We left them with instructions, including no TV—we would feel the back of the television on our return, and if it was hot we would know they had not complied with that rule—watch out for the little siblings, and above all, don't drive the car. I believe that Shawn had a learner's permit at that time, but not a license, and we didn't want them out driving around in our absence.

We only got to the edge of town before Parley realized he had forgotten his saw, and we immediately turned around to pick it up before we headed up the mountain. We turned on to our street, and there in the middle of Lassen Lane, just out in front of our driveway, was our family car.

Shawn was in the driver's seat, desperately trying to get the stalled car started. In those days an inexperienced driver could flood the engine and cause the car to stall, and that was probably what had happened. Shawn knew she was in trouble. She was probably also very afraid that her dad was going to yell at her; maybe ground her for a month.

She looked very small behind that steering wheel as Parley got out of the pickup truck and walked up to her door. He motioned for her to roll down the window, and when she did, he uttered the words that have become family lore: "What's the matter, hon? Can't get the damned thing started?"

He didn't use curse words often, and Shawn was probably not sure if she was in even worse trouble than she expected. But this was Parley's way of breaking the tension. He told her to scoot over, and he expertly got the car to start right up, and pulled it into the driveway.

There were no further words of censure; no grounding; no punishment. It was another love lesson for me. Don't give a scolding to someone who really needs a hug. He knew that Shawn was very hard on herself and didn't need to have an airing of her faults; rather she needed to know that she had a dad who loved her.

I learned that physical affection is an important aspect of love. Physical affection was not part of my childhood, and I was, in my turn, physically reserved. When I picture Parley, even now, he is lying on the floor on his back. He has one of more of the kids, or grandkids, cradled in one of his huge, muscular arms, and he is telling them a story and probably how beautiful they are, how proud he is of them, and how much he loves them.

If no child is available, then there is a golden retriever, and he is probably telling them a story, how beautiful they are, how proud he is of them, and how much he loves them!

Because I had grown up in such an undemonstrative home, it took me awhile to get used to Parley's desire to be physically close all the time. Even if he was just working on something, he liked to have me by him, with a hand on his arm or his shoulder.

One day I remember going out to the driveway where Parley was sitting behind the steering wheel of his truck and I was standing outside the window, and we were talking to someone. After a few minutes, he reached out through the window and put his arm around me. That brought me great happiness and I felt a closeness that made me feel special. I loved going to church more after I married Parley. He always had me pulled close to him when we were in worship services, and I loved that.

One of the important love lessons I have learned is that love needs not burn out and die of boredom. I learned that people who love each other can grow together, and that the best years of a marriage can happen decades later. This was certainly true for me, and we turned to each other with the truest of love in the last years of Parley's life. The frequency of the words,

"I love you," ebbed and flowed in our marriage, but toward the end, when I knew I was going to lose him, I couldn't tell him enough how much I loved him, and the wonderful things that he was to me.

Parley told me every day that he loved me. He told me almost every day that I was beautiful. He noticed things that I wore, and he cared. He told me that he liked, or didn't like things. That led to some very humorous "pants burning parties."

I am a creature of habit and comfort. I would get into a habit of wearing the same worn, comfortable but hideously ugly clothes all the time, especially pants. One day he took a look at my awful outfit, and said, "Today, we're going to have a pants burning party!" He encouraged me take out all my worn-out pants and we burned them in the backyard.

Parley taught me about loving others. I would never be able to count the amount of times he would arrive home after church on Sunday with a new family that he had invited to dinner. I learned to always make enough food for a crowd, because there would nearly always be one.

We were never rich, but Parley always had enough to share. I could not count on two hands the times someone in need would find a plain white envelope filled with enough crisp, new hundred-dollar bills to pay their rent or their tuition, fix their car or pay a doctor's bill. I tried, recently, to remember the names of every troubled child we fostered through the years. I stopped at thirty, but there may have been more.

I can't count the number of love letters Parley wrote me—a few, before we were married, but many more, in all the years after. I learned so many love lessons from Parley, and I tried to put them into practice. While he was alive, I was able to live rather quietly in the shelter of his big, beautiful and loving personality. It was safe and cozy there, and because we were such a team, all the love he shared was mine, too. I could tell myself that "we" were very loving.

It was only after he passed away that I realized I was going to be here for awhile longer, and that there was no "we" are very loving; not anymore. It was time for me to dust off all the love lessons and put them into practice. It has taken me the fifteen years since he went on before me, to be able to say "I" am very loving. It took me all ninety years to get to the point where I could make a reel and share my love for the Savior, and to share my love for my neighbors—for *you*.

I am, perhaps, a late bloomer, but I am so grateful for the love lessons. I am so grateful for the most extraordinary teacher of them. I am so grateful for a Heavenly Father who led me, sometimes dragged me, but most often carried me—down a broken road to find my Parley. I want you to know that being mostly love, as I am now, is a beautiful thing. I highly recommend it. And in case you have forgotten... I love you!

Sandy and Belle

The week that one of my daughters was born,
Parley brought home our first golden retriever. Parley
loved his kids and he loved his dogs—not necessarily

in that order. Over the course of our married life we
had eleven golden retrievers.

We visited a friend in Mt. Shasta who had two
beautiful retrievers—sisters named Sandy and Belle.

The friend told Parley that he was going to give Sandy to him, and Parley was absolutely thrilled. Before the friend relinquished Sandy, he took us both out and showed us all the amazing tricks those gorgeous dogs could do.

He had the two dogs sit quietly, and he would give a command to either Belle or Sandy, and the pair would listen attentively. If he gave a command to Belle, Sandy would not move, and vice versa. Meanwhile, the dog he commanded would race to perform the trick or task. Belle and Sandy were amazing. He would command Sandy to go get a ball and she would run off to find a ball. She was perfectly obedient and understood so many things. So we were excited to get her home.

The next morning we went out to give her a workout, and Parley said, "Sit." *She did not.* Then he told her "Come, Sandy." She laid there, just looking at him. He tried louder, quieter, firmer and even offering treats. Nothing helped. Everything he commanded, she just looked at him. Parley was crushed that he got this dog that would not listen to him. He took Sandy back to the friend and told him that he was sorry, but it seemed that the dog was broken.

Parley's friend listened with concern, but upon hearing all the things we had tried, he started to laugh. He blew our minds when he told us: "That's not Sandy," (indicating our dog); "That's Belle."

I will never forget what a different experience it was, bringing Sandy home that second time. She was absolutely perfect. What a loving, well-trained dog she was. We used to joke that we didn't have to hire a babysitter, because she thought that was her sworn duty. We also learned an important lesson that day: If things don't seem to be working, *always check and make sure you brought home the right dog!*

Chapter 17
Acts of Love

Before Parley passed away from cancer, he wanted me to have a golden retriever to keep me company when he was gone. We had spent some time without a dog, so Parley kept his eyes out for one. He found a litter of purebred retrievers a couple of hours away, and he drove us out to look. There were two pens of puppies, and the owner recommended one particular puppy, and we agreed to return two weeks later when the puppy could leave its mother. On the appointed day, the owner had the puppy ready for us, but Parley told her that he had changed his mind. He indicated a little ball of fluff in one of the pens, and told the owner that *that* was our dog. That was how we brought home Roxy Ann.

Parley told me Roxy Ann was my dog, because he didn't want me to feel alone after he passed away. At the time, I wasn't sure how I felt about that. Roxy was an irresistible little puppy—but I was not the one in the family who loved the dogs—that was Parley. Roxy was the last in a line of many golden retrievers that had been a part of our family, but they had always been Parley's dogs, not mine. Parley was so sick by that point, however, that I would have done anything for him. Every day I woke up and thought about what I could do to make him happy.

Parley lived for about three more months after we got the puppy. His skin was terribly thin and fragile by then, and Roxy was all fur and little needle-sharp teeth. He loved her so much, though, that I would still put her up in the bed with him because it made him so happy. She drew blood on his hands and arms almost every time but he didn't care. After he passed away and she was truly my dog, I adjusted to being a "dog person" very quickly and I loved her. She loved me too. I soon discovered that one of the gifts of having a loving pet like Roxy was that when I would arrive home after being anywhere, instead of coming home to a house that was missing Parley, I came home to her, and she was so delighted to see me every single time.

Roxy was beautiful and a wonderful companion for me. In her earlier years I took her for a lot of hikes and daily walks. As I aged and it became harder for me to keep up that exercise, Roxy Ann aged too. She was my beautiful friend for eleven years, and when her health failed and she died, it absolutely broke my heart. We had had so many dogs, and when they died it was sad but they were not my dogs and I felt

detached from them. Not so with Roxy Ann; I felt like my world had closed in again, without her in it.

One day a month or two later, my friend Kristi stopped by my home. She was accompanied by her little 12-year-old golden doodle. "This is Lulu," Kristi said, "and we are going to share her." I was puzzled at first, but she explained that Lulu was to be my dog, except when her kids were visiting and wanted to see her and then she would take her back for a few days.

Lulu was adorable, adaptable and well-behaved. She was happy to be at my house, and equally happy to spend the a few days Kristi's house. I love Lulu and she loves me. She has made the last two years very much more special for me.

But Lulu is not the real story here; the real story is Kristi. She took to heart the admonition of the Lord to "bear one another's burdens." She thought about what I needed, and then figured out a way to care for me. True joy comes when we take care of each other.

I think there may be many who read this who feel lonely and isolated. You may feel that there is no one who looks after you. I want you to know that no matter how alone you may feel, you are a child of God and you are never alone or unloved.

I remember from my "lone pine" days how I felt like I had to do everything on my own, and I often worried that I would not be okay. If you have some of those feelings, I hope that you will reach out and begin with small steps to surround yourself with people who uplift you and support you; people who need your care, and who will give you that loving care in return.

In the past year that I have been on hospice care, my daughter has stayed to look after me, and in November, she scheduled a night to herself in a cabin in the mountains. When she let people know of her plans to be gone for about 18 hours, many friends offered to come and stay with me, but I didn't need that. She had laid out all my medications for the hours she would be gone, and I was looking forward to some quiet time to myself too.

She returned home to find that I had received many visitors who were anxious to look after me in her absence. In particular one of her own friends, Cecily, had stopped by to drop off some music that she needed, and had left a kind note and a meal of potato soup and rolls. It looked delicious, but for  my daughter, it was more than that. With the soup and rolls, she had left homemade strawberry jam, a tiny dish of butter… and a sweet little butter knife.

Why did she leave a butter knife? Obviously we have knives here. Probably even a butter knife. But for my daughter, that little knife was like a secret message, whispering that she was special and important. Cecily didn't just want her to be fed; she wanted her to be cared for. The butter knife may seem so small as to be insignificant, but it elevated a simple act of service to an act of love. How beautiful it would be; how Christlike, even, to elevate our every pursuit in this way.

There have been times in my life when I have battled illness or adversity, either for myself or for a family member, and a well-meaning friend has offered the words: "Let me know if there is anything I can do." I must confess that I have uttered those words, myself, on more than one occasion, and while the sentiment may be heartfelt, the words themselves have but little practical use.

Kristi could have come to me after Roxy Ann died and said some kind words. She could have hugged me and said, "Let me know if there's anything I can do." But she elevated what would have been been an act of service—visiting me with kind words— and instead performed an act of love, by giving me the precious gift of her own little dog. Do you see how much more powerful that is?

There is no better example than the Savior—in all things— but especially regarding how we should care for each other. He acted, not out of a desire to be seen and praised, but out of a deep and loving compassion, and it is that compassion that we need in order to truly love our neighbors as ourselves.

I hope that instead of giving acts of service, we might learn how to offer acts of love. I hope that we can be the ones who show up to weed flower beds like my friend Karla, or show up with a mousetrap when a tired friend hears tiny feet in the garage at night, or simply listen with sympathy when someone needs to be heard.

I hope that we stand up for our kids in a parent-teacher conference and that we refuse to hear hurtful gossip and that if someone is in need, that we stop to listen with our hearts to find out what is needed and freely give it in love. I hope we never say "Let me know if there's anything I can do," ever again. I hope we take care of each other as the Savior cares for each of us. I love you!

Chapter 18
Love and the "Yes" Mom

"Making the decision to have a child — it's momentous. It is to decide forever to have your heart go walking around outside your body."
—Elizabeth Stone

I love children, and so much of the joy that I have experienced in my long life has resulted from the incomparable experience of motherhood, but it has also been complicated, challenging, frustrating and even heartbreaking. This is such an important topic to me, and it deserves a certain immediacy which is difficult for me because it has been so many decades since I was a parent to small humans.

For this reason, I hope you will understand me drawing heavily on my daughter's much more recent experiences. Most of the words in this book are hers, as she has done all the writing, so it seems natural to lean on her wisdom here, as it is the same I would hope to impart. With the understanding that this is a team effort, let's talk about parenthood.

I almost didn't get stretch marks. I was nine months' pregnant with my first baby. Forty weeks. My skin was stretched taut over my large, beautiful abdomen. I didn't see any of the tiny, light pink, almost irridescent lines that I thought of as stretch marks. I was almost home free. All I had to do was the unthinkable act of pushing a baby out of my body, and then I could spring back into shape like a rubber band released from tension. *Easy.*

But it turned out there were lessons to be learned. My firstborn was reluctant to emerge from the luxury apartment that was my uterus. He exercised his option to extend the lease— for twelve long days. And just

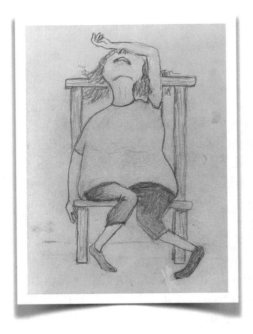

two days after the due date, the first stretch marks appeared.

These were not the small, barely noticeable pink lines I had previously associated with stretch marks. No, these were something out of a horror movie. I didn't feel anything different. I couldn't have told you when or how it happened. All I knew was that one day I had a pale, smooth belly, and that the next day I caught sight of myself in the mirror and gasped when I saw the long, wicked, inch-high red slash marks beginning just above my belly button. Each day it seemed there were new ones.

When my nine-pound baby boy finally vacated the premises and everything slowly began to shrink back to its former dimensions, those stretch marks remained like deep lacerations in my skin, and I felt that what remained of my once-flat and supple midsection now resembled a topographical map of somewhere inhospitable.

Over time, those marks faded to that slightly irridescent palest of pinks that I now know is part of the healing process, not how they look when they first happen. The skin on my belly will never be smooth again, but I don't mind that particular reminder of those days. It was part of the lesson of stretch marks.

Just as my belly had to stretch beyond all reason to accommodate that baby, my whole existence had to stretch to accommodate motherhood. The dramatic red slashes on my skin were certainly no more dramatic than the figurative stretch marks on my life. I had thought I was confident, patient, kind and loving before. But when that baby emerged, if there had been smooth, perfect skin over my soul, that singular experience would have stretched it past its very limits.

I got a few small stretch marks in subsequent pregnancies, but never many. I used to think to myself that the damage had already been done. But maybe it would have been more accurate to tell myself that *growth had already occurred*. And yes, of course there was still room for growth, but never again did there have to be that visceral tearing of either my skin or my soul. I had been forever altered; my capacity expanded; the capacity for love, unselfishness, patience, wisdom, happiness, mental toughness; even for pain tolerance.

As I think about how we should approach this sacred responsibility of caring for children, my mind is always drawn to the Savior, and how much love he had for them. In the book of Mark in the New Testament, Chapter 10, we read of His ministry, and how some parents brought their children to him to be blessed. His disciples tried to send the parents away so that the exhausted Savior could rest, but he corrected them, saying: *"Suffer the little children to come unto me, and forbid them not: for of such is the kingdom of God. Verily I say unto you, Whosoever shall not receive the kingdom of God as a little child, he shall not enter therein." And he took them up in his arms, put his hands upon them, and blessed them.*

It is important to understand that when the savior said "Suffer the little children," the word suffer meant "allow." We never want our children to suffer in the painful sense of the word. But allowing them to be near us, allowing them to be children, allowing them to make decisions for themselves, especially as they grow—those things are vital.

Being a parent can be overwhelming. We must teach them correct principles and then let them make decisions for themselves. We must be consistent. We must be loving. We must keep them safe. All of this must be accomplished in the midst of what often feels like chaos.

My daughter relates this story of the "Yes Mom": *Once upon a time I was a young mom with a wolf pack of small, feral boys. I loved it. It was the best thing ever. And I mean that with all my heart. Nothing better. Sometimes I felt like I was living out a dream of being Wendy bird with the lost boys from Peter Pan.*

But while It may have been the best thing ever, it was also the most exhausting thing ever. They were so smart and imaginative and active… and exhausting. I found myself falling into patterns that I didn't like. I was becoming the dreaded NO MOM.

It almost didn't matter what the question was: if I heard the words, "Mom, can we...." the answer was "No. Whatever it is, no." And whatever I would see them doing, that was also more than likely a NO.

Granted, these were busy times. I also had a pretty crazy life aside from feral-boy-raising. I had a busy schedule accompanying choral groups at the local high school, a slew of piano students and a graphic design business with a few rather large clients. Everyone always needed something and my husband made me stand in front of the mirror and practice smiling ruefully and saying the phrase "Oh, I wish I could" over and over so that I could learn to say no politely to the many requests that always seemed to come my way.

But then, why was it that I was finding it so easy to be the No Mom all the time? Maybe it was survival mode. But that wasn't it, entirely. What it really came down to was an attitude. And I didn't like my attitude and I didn't like that I was so willing to part with all these pieces of myself for good causes, but when it came to the best cause of all, I was being stingy and self-protective. So I decided to make a change. I still kept doing many of the activities. But I got a lot better at smiling ruefully and saying "Oh, I wish I could." I made a pact with myself that when it came to my kids, I would say YES as often as I possibly could.

This was a subtle shift. It felt big to me, but I doubt the boys, who are mostly grown now, would *remember that happening. And with any luck, they don't remember the tired 20-something "No Mom" at all. We got to have adventures and we got to enjoy each other and they got to learn to make decisions and feel free to become who they were supposed to be. We all did.*

This isn't a parenting tutorial, but I love this idea of the Yes Mom, and I challenge you to try it; not just for kids, nor even for grandkids, but try it for *yourself*. Try to tell yourself yes as often as you possibly can. Find excuses to *do* things, rather than finding excuses why *not* to do things. Yes, it's a subtle shift, but an important one just the same.

The last thing I would like to talk about with regards to parenthood, is communication. I think sometimes that we believe our job as parents is to tell our kids *all the things*. We believe that teaching them means telling them everything. But communication isn't about doing all the talking, is it? Communication implies that we commune; that we exchange ideas. It is perhaps more important for us to listen to what our children have to tell us, than it is for us to tell them what we want them to know.

When my kids were young, I thought it was important to give them household chores to do, to teach them responsibility and get them to help out. It was really easy for some of the chores to fall to the same child every time.

So it was with my youngest, Paul. By the time he was eleven or twelve years old, it became his job to take out the kitchen waste and put it in the trash can outside. After the first many times he did this task, I began to take for granted that it was his job.

One night after I called for him loudly to take out the trash, he stomped in with a lot of frustration. He said, "I'm starting to think that my name isn't just Paul anymore, because all you ever call me is "Garbage, Paul!" We laughed at that then, and sometimes we still do… but it was a reminder to me that my kids deserved respect and appreciation.

Creating an environment of safety, where our children feel they can tell us things, is one of the best gifts that we can give them, and that ability to be honest will help to address or even avoid so many of the problems that can injure our children. Simply by listening to our children, we establish ourselves as allies for them, and as the years fly by faster than we want them to, we can find so much joy in their company.

The other aspect of communication that I have found to have a huge impact, is the way we speak to our children, and indeed, to all our family members. I like to ask this question: What is your kindness level? Many times if we are talking to friends or even strangers, we are careful to address them respectfully and kindly, but when we talk to our own children, we change that respectful tone to one of impatience, frustration or even anger.

I would invite you to think about famous last words. My mother lived to be 100. She was tiny, beautiful and elegant, even at that age. She lived on her own well Into her nineties, and when she was 100 she lived with Parley and me.

One afternoon a few months into her 101st year, she told me, "Kay, I'm dying." I calmly explained to her: "You're not dying. We just took you to the doctor last week and he said you were strong and doing great." I then asked her, "Are you in pain? Would you like me to get you an aspirin?" Mom shrugged and said "Alright," almost as if to appease me. I gave her the aspirin, and she swallowed it with a small glass of water. Then she laid down and two minutes later she died.

There are a lot of possible lessons from this experience, but for the purposes of this chapter, think about my famous last words: My mother told me she was dying and I told her... *to take an aspirin.* I wish I had not responded dismissively; maybe even a little impatiently. I wish I had taken that very singular opportunity to tell my mom that I loved her; to impress upon her what a wonderful mother she was. I wish I had expressed gratitude for everything she had done for me.

I know she will forgive me for those famous last words. I will see her soon enough and we will have a laugh about that. But in contrast, I think of my granddaughter and *her* famous last words, even though, like my mom and me, she didn't know at the time that they would be her last.

Two and a half years into Cambria's fight with cancer, she had had a stem cell transplant, and it was by far the most difficult time of her treatments. They killed every bit of her immune system in preparation for that procedure and they provided her family with a four-inch thick binder of all the rules associated with her recovery. She was on a zero-bacteria regimen. No fresh fruits or vegetables. Water had to come from clean disposable water bottles.

Six weeks post-transplant, and after only being released from the hospital a week earlier, she got sick. It was a common virus that was going around. My daughter caught it at the same time and was starting to get feverish and achy even as she sat next to Cambria's bed in the children's hospital emergency room. But it was different for Cambria. Her body had nothing with which to fight off that virus.

In the emergency room that day, her oxygen saturation was hovering in the 80% range. You wouldn't have guessed that because she was sitting up and talking and laughing. Nurses and doctors from oncology heard she was there and several stopped in to talk to her and tell her about some show they had watched or laugh at a joke she would tell. She had a big, booming laugh that could be heard all through the emergency room.

After several hours the doctor said that they would definitely have to admit her because it was so dangerous for her to be sick. Cambria told her mom to go home and rest and the staff would take care of her admission. Her dad had brought up her favorite blanket and some bottles of water so her mom ran out to the car to bring them in to her. They agreed to speak later after she was admitted.

As my daughter was walking out to the car, Cambria called out across the emergency room, "I love you, Mom!" And Victoria called back, "I love you too!" *Those were their famous last words.* At 2:00 am they got a phone call. The intensive care staff had had to cut off her clothes and induce a coma so that they could intubate her. She had a fever of 105 degrees and had been in respiratory arrest. She was on life support for two more weeks but she never regained consciousness.

My daughter didn't know when she walked out of the emergency room that day that those would be their last words, but it means everything to her that they were loving and happy words. So I ask you again about your communication with your loved ones: What is your kindness level?

Especially when it comes to your children, my prayer is that your last words are on the far distant horizon, but I hope that every time you speak, you treat it as if it could be your last time. Make it matter. Make it kind. Praise and inspire. Never belittle or criticize, even when you have to correct them. Love them as generously as you possibly can. If you are blessed to be a parent, I hope it brings you the joy that it has brought me. Family is everything. I love you!

Chapter 19
Love and Amber

In the quiet misty morning
When the moon has gone to bed
When the sparrows stop their singing
And the sky is clear and red
When the summer's ceased its gleaming
When the corn is past its prime
When adventure's lost its meaning
I'll be homeward bound in time.

Bind me not to the pasture;
Chain me not to the plow
Set me free to find my calling
And I'll return to you somehow.

Maybe its just like they say—before you die, your whole life flashes before your eyes. That is what has happened for me, writing this book. I told you it wouldn't be a biography, and it really wasn't, was it? I didn't tell you all the times I had babies or moved here or there. I left out many tragedies, triumphs, ups, downs, *all-over-the-places*. Instead I chose to include the many love lessons I have learned. But my whole life flashed before my own eyes. And it was a pretty great show.

I like the expression, "the days are long but the years are short." That seems very true to me. Something that I noticed when Parley passed away was that *time stood still*. It was like a black hole phenomenon from a sci-fi book, where the closer you get to the phenomenon, the more time slows, so that what seems like seconds to you is days, or even years to those who have not been pulled into it.

That seems like a pretty good analogy in my mind, because I was pulled into the vortex of Parley's death; which wasn't some horrible pit of unimaginable suffering like you might imagine. In fact, I wasn't the slightest bit sad for *him*; he had suffered terrible health issues for several years, and I could only be glad he didn't have to be in pain any longer. Not only that, but I have faith that we will be reunited after this life and that means everything to me. But it was instead a time of missing him; numbness and a sort of exhaustion.

After his passing I was, either consciously or subconsciously, using all my powers to slow time. I couldn't reverse it and bring him back, but by freezing time, it kept him… *recent*… as though he was just here.

Even now, I can close my eyes and picture Parley. He was a journeyman glazier, but for a few years we lived on and worked a ranch that had been in his family since he was young. It was a heavenly place with 200 acres of apple trees. There was a garden with rich, black soil that would reveal a crop of obsidian arrowheads after a hard rain. It was apparently sown over indigenous campsites or, maybe more likely, an ancient battleground, and it was like a treasure hunt to look for the glistening black arrowheads winking in the sunlight. In my mind's eye, I can see Parley scoop up a big handful of that soil and hold it up to my nose. "Just smell this," he would say with his infectious enthusiasm, as though it was the best fragrance in the world.

The problem is that no matter how successful you are at freezing time—and we can all be— think of the parent whose child has gone away to college and they keep his room exactly the same so it can seem as though he never left— but no matter how hard you try, time only freezes *for you*. The rest of the world refuses to tarry with you for even a few short seconds.

You may *will* time to stand still around you, but people are still laughing at jokes and getting new jobs and their first puppy and failing tests at school and falling in love and getting sunburnt and playing video games and finding out they're pregnant and laughing at a show on TV.

I observed that even others who knew and loved Parley, and there were so many— managed to stay out of the vortex of the black hole. They missed him but time didn't stop for them; there was a small slowdown but then they achieved escape velocity.

I didn't ever reach escape velocity. Instead I traveled through the wormhole to the other side. The only way out was through. Time has resumed, but I still see certain things from that frozen perspective. It is as though I am looking through beautiful golden amber that has preserved a tiny insect since prehistory.

Preserving memories as though in golden amber can be so bittersweet. In it, Parley is still healthy in that garden on the ranch. My granddaughter Cambria is a teenager forever in the amber glass, while her friends go on to universities and marry and get jobs and have babies. It is a sad and lovely thing. *It is both.*

I recall a particularly beautiful fall sunrise from last October. I could see only the reflection of it from my bed and I thought to myself that I had time to close my eyes for a few more minutes and then I would get up and bask in its beauty. Ten minutes later I opened my eyes to see sun streaming through the sheer curtains of my room and all the beautiful colors had gone. I had tried to freeze time but it had gone on ahead all around me.

Time doesn't stop, and soon it will be *my* turn to pass into the next life. I will see my Parley again, and Cambria. I will see my beloved parents and my brother Ted. I don't want you to be sad for me. My love for Parley has beckoned me; guided me, even; it has given meaning to my final years and without it, my off-her-rocker adventure would not have been possible.

I feel light in my soul, and even butterflies at the thought of our reunion which must come very soon. You won't have to preserve me in amber, because I am leaving you this book, which I hope is a vibrant account of my journey to become "mostly love, now."

In May and June of 2023, I began to experience some lightheadedness. I fainted a couple of times, and made everyone worry over me, which is something I never have liked to do. My doctor said that my blood pressure was low, and that was what was causing the fainting.

I had been eating more carefully, and we attributed the resulting weight loss to that change. The doctor eliminated a couple of medications I had been taking for high blood pressure. He mentioned that he also wanted to check on my heart function, especially since I had struggled with covid a few months earlier. He attached monitors to me that I would wear twenty-four hours a day for a month and then send in for evaluation. I felt much better, and didn't expect that they would find anything on the heart monitor.

I was wrong about that. In July I went back to the doctor to discuss the results of that test, and he told me that I had severe aortic stenosis. I was in heart failure. He referred me to a cardiologist to discuss a possible procedure that would help me. As I sat there in his office and he spoke to me about options, I did not really hear any of them. It was as though his lips were moving but nothing was coming out. I only heard two words out of the entire conversation: "You're dying."

My daughter was on an extended trip and my 19-year-old grandson was staying with me and caring for me. He drove me home from the appointment and I didn't tell him what the doctor said. I didn't tell anyone. I went home and settled in to die.

I was convinced it was going to happen imminently. Friends visited. My grandson cooked me whatever I asked for to eat. Whether it was shrimp tacos or baked spaghetti, he would look up a recipe and make it for me. I knew I was about to die, and I was a little scared and a little sad, but I was also a little relieved and determined to enjoy my last days.

When a couple of weeks went by, and I hadn't actually died, I decided to call my daughter on her trip and let her know that I was dying. She had the nerve to not be devastated by my news! Instead she told me I needed to go back to the doctor and listen again to all the options he had given me, and that I should stop feeling sorry for myself and find something better to focus on. She told me I should make a reel for Off Her Rocker, make an appointment with a cardiologist, and not plan on dying until she could get home to help me. I found that I actually

felt a lot better, once I had a plan of action.

My grandson insisted on going in with me to the doctor for that second visit. It was a good thing, because while all I still heard was "You're dying," he heard all the other things the doctor said, and could remind me of them after we left. What followed in the next two months were a lot of ups and downs, as I was first told that I was a great candidate for a TAVR procedure, which would correct the aortic stenosis, but then subsequent tests revealed a regurgitant mitral valve, meaning that I was no longer a candidate for the minimally invasive procedure.

What I was left with, by September, was a dire prognosis, hospice care, and the final love lesson I had to learn. My loving Heavenly Father had one last requirement for me in my mortal probation, and it's one I thought I had already mastered: *I had to endure to the end.*

A dear friend and former heart surgeon sat across from me and told me that my prognosis was not a pleasant prospect. I would struggle more and more with shortness of breath. My heart function would gradually wind down. It would likely be very miserable. This was not how I wanted my life to end, and I struggled against it. At this point I didn't want to freeze any time. It needed to fly so that I could just pass quietly and be done.

It has been a year now since that initial diagnosis of aortic stenosis. These days, I have almost as many weak days as strong days, but because of hospice care and comfort medications, I do not experience much at all of the misery I feared. The hospice nurses who visit weekly say that my heart sounds very much like a washing machine. I stopped receiving my monthly eye injections, so my macular degeneration has advanced and I am nearly blind.

But I plant flowers in my back yard. I wear pretty dresses that make me happy. I can barely see where my brush is going, but I still make small watercolor paintings in a little leather-bound journal. I have found the stamina to spend many hours talking about my experiences so that my daughter could do the writing for this book. I video-chat with children and grandchildren and great-grandchildren. And most importantly, I bask in the love that I feel from my Heavenly Father and His son, my Savior, Jesus Christ.

This love lesson of enduring to the end— it has not been my easiest, but it is not because I am in physical discomfort as I feared. It is because I have been impatient and I thought I knew what was best for me. *I thought I knew the ending.* I turns out I didn't, and I still don't. But I have stopped trying to either freeze time or speed it up.

I am humbled to know that Heavenly Father's plan for me included sharing my testimony even in this, my tenth decade on this planet. I think back to a year ago, and I didn't even know then that I would have a book now to share with you. I have just experienced a crazy, amazing roller coaster ride of a year. I am filled with gratitude for the joy that has come from enduring to the end.

The real lesson was the pure, lovely, simple reminder that even in a tired body with some failing parts, I am really just a child of my Heavenly Father, and I am beloved by my elder brother, Jesus Christ, who uplifts me, atones for me, loves and protects me. I bear testimony to you that he knows each of us personally and that even in my darkest, scariest hours,

I feel myself wrapped in His loving arms and I know that I am okay; it truly is well with my soul.

I love you so much—all of you, my brothers and sisters. I want you to understand that as much as I feel this great and abiding love for you, it is but a drop in the ocean to the love that the Savior feels for each of you. I testify that we are not here just to "get through this," but that we exist to feel joy. I hope that if this book has done anything at all, that it has made you feel loved, and that it has stoked your desire to turn to the source of that love: even your Savior, Jesus Christ.

I am grateful for my ninety-two years of beautiful, precious time. I keep countless happy things preserved in the amber of my life, and time has turned them all bittersweet and golden for me to treasure. I love those memories but I wouldn't truly freeze time… and I can't, and won't stay. The days are long; the years are short; and I have so much to see. God will surely be with you until we meet again. I love you.

> *If you find it's me you're missing*
> *If you're hoping I'll return*
> *To your thoughts, I'll soon be listening*
> *And in the road, I'll stop and turn*
>
> *Then the wind will set me racing*
> *As my journey nears its end*
> *And the path I'll be retracing*
> *When I'm homeward bound again.*
> —Homeward Bound by Marta Keen

Afterword
All love, now.

"Take courage, dear one."
—C.S. Lewis

I knew there had to be a book. There were nights where I could not sleep for hours on end, and I felt like the Lord was telling me that there had to be a book, and that it was urgent because I would not be here for much longer. But while I have written two or three books, they were more along the lines of personal history. This had to be something very special, and I have come to a time in my life where I don't have the stamina, the eyesight, or the cleverness that I once did for such things. I am not capable of putting together any kind of a book, now— let alone one that would possess a bit of magic, as I believe this one does.

Fortunately for me, and for you, I have in my home, caring for me on a daily basis, someone extraordinary. My daughter Victoria is such a lovely writer. I am one of many who have long loved her essays and blogs. She has the ability to look at life and experiences, even the most difficult ones, without deep judgment, as though the past is a friend, and not a lost opportunity. It allows readers space to take what they need from her words.

In preparing for this book, I have laid bare all of my innermost thoughts and feelings. I have shared things that I love, and I have shared things for which I have carried shame and regret all these years. It fell to

Victoria to take all those things and make them into something beautiful; something *more*. She taught me to forgive myself and leave the regret behind. She showed me that it was important to share the imperfections so that others would realize that they were not so alone.

The result is this book that entirely represents me and says all the things I wanted to say, with the addition of Victoria's own profound wisdom, and lovelier words than I could have written for myself. Victoria's underlying theme is always redemption, and I feel like she was able to express that on my behalf, and for that I am entirely grateful.

I wanted this book to be a lovely sort of goodbye. I want you to know that your love—whether you are my family, or one of my thousands of friends who have left incredibly kind, uplifting comments on my instagram posts—*your* love, has sustained me and lifted me up. You have made all the difference for an old lady who is, as we have previously established, *off her rocker*.

I think there will be many times after I have passed away, where I will look back here across that veil, and I will wish that I could just come back and put my arm around you and tell you that you're going to be okay. I would tell you that you need to worry less and love more, and have joy in your life. There will be times when you will lose faith. You live in a precarious time. Doubt will whisper to your mind.

When those times come, I want you to "take courage, dear one," as C.S. Lewis wrote. Don't give in to those doubts. If you need some faith, please borrow some of mine. That is what this book is for. It's the hug from beyond the veil; the reminder that you will be okay; the bit of faith you need so that you can continue to believe. Lean on my testimony when you need to. The Savior's love is abiding and eternal, and you must never lose sight of that perfect hope in Him.

With all my love and gratitude,
Katherine

Works Cited

Cherry, Jane. "Kisses" by permission of her children.

Corbutt, Neal. Newspaper excerpt.

Hayden, Carruth. Excerpt from *Scrambled Eggs & Whiskey: Poems 1991-1995*, Copper Canyon Press, Port Townsend, WA, 1996, p. 35.
Keen, Marta. Excerpts from "Homeward Bound".

Magee, John Gillespie. Excerpt from "High Flight." *Letter To Parents*, Library of Congress, Washington, DC, 1941.

Saunders, George. Quote from convocation speech at Syracuse University for the class of 2013.

Wilcox, Ella Wheeler. "Solitude".

Made in United States
Troutdale, OR
08/25/2024

22297104R00120